PRAISE FOR PETER BATES

From *"The Complete FinOps Handbook:"*

If you're not sure of the scope of FinOps, and need to learn quickly to give a good impression when dealing with FinOps professionals, then this book is exactly right for that. It covers all the important aspects of the profession, including budgeting and forecasting, financial reporting, cost management, financial analysis, financial modeling, risk management, treasury management, and compliance.

— T. C. MAN

This book provides great insight on the financial operations skills required to run a successful business. I definitely recommend this book!

— P. B. GRACE

This book has all you need for techniques on operating financials. It has all tools need to organize and run your daily operations smoothly, optimize and run your risk management, budgeting, financial analysis and analytics. If this is the career path you're taking or you're working in the field, this book has all the tools you need to steer you to the right path.

— R. FERRARA

D1720167

LEARNING THE ART OF CLOUD FINOPS

LEARNING THE ART OF CLOUD FINOPS

STRATEGIES, TOOLS, AND BEST PRACTICES FOR
FINANCIAL SUCCESS IN THE CLOUD ERA

DIGITAL FINANCE

PETER BATES

Book
Bound Studios

To the trailblazers and innovators in the world of finance who have embraced the power of cloud computing, and to those who aspire to do the same. This book is dedicated to your pursuit of financial excellence and your unwavering commitment to adapt, evolve, and thrive in the ever-changing landscape of financial operations. May the insights and strategies shared within these pages guide you towards a secure, efficient, and prosperous future in cloud finance.

In the age of cloud, financial success is shaped by those who dare to ride the winds of change, transforming the intangible into a wealth of possibilities.

— UNKNOWN

CONTENTS

INTRODUCTION TO CLOUD FINANCIAL OPERATIONS

In the ever-evolving world of finance, the emergence of **cloud computing** has heralded a new era of unprecedented possibilities, opportunities, and challenges. The dawn of this new financial era has brought with it a paradigm shift in the way businesses and financial professionals manage, analyze, and leverage data to drive growth, streamline operations, and foster innovation. As the sun rises on this new landscape, it is crucial for financial professionals to adapt, embrace, and harness the power of cloud financial operations to stay ahead of the curve and thrive in an increasingly competitive and dynamic environment.

The advent of cloud computing has not only transformed the way financial data is stored and accessed but has also redefined the very essence of financial operations. Gone are the days of cumbersome spreadsheets, siloed data, and time-consuming manual processes. In their place, we now have real-time access to vast amounts of data, seamless integration of financial systems, and powerful analytical tools that enable financial professionals to make informed decisions **quickly and accurately**.

As we stand at the cusp of this new financial era, it is essential to recognize that the cloud is not merely a technological innovation but a catalyst for change that has the potential to revolutionize the entire financial industry. From small businesses to multinational corporations, cloud financial operations are leveling the playing field, empowering organizations to harness the power of data-driven insights, and fostering a culture of agility, innovation, and collaboration.

In this book, we will delve into the world of cloud financial operations, exploring its origins, its impact on the financial industry, and the myriad ways in which financial professionals can leverage this transformative technology to drive success in the cloud age. By understanding the intricacies of cloud financial operations and embracing the opportunities it presents, you will be well-equipped to navigate the complexities of this new era and emerge as a trailblazer in the world of finance. So, let us embark on this exciting journey together as we usher in the dawn of a new financial era and chart a course toward a future of limitless potential.

Tracing the Roots of Cloud Computing in Finance

The journey of cloud computing in finance has been fascinating, marked by rapid advancements and transformative innovations. To truly appreciate the impact of cloud financial operations, it is essential to understand the origins of cloud computing and its evolution within the financial industry.

The concept of cloud computing dates back to the *1960s* when computer scientist *John McCarthy* proposed the idea of time-sharing, which allowed multiple users to access a single computer simultaneously. This concept laid the foundation for the development of cloud computing as we know it today. However, it wasn't until the late *1990s* and early *2000s* that cloud computing began to gain traction, thanks to the advent of the internet and the increasing need for businesses to store and manage vast amounts of data.

As the internet and technology continued to evolve, so did the financial industry's need for more efficient and cost-effective ways to manage their operations. The traditional methods of maintaining on-premise data centers and IT infrastructure were **no longer sustainable,** as they required significant investments in hardware, software, and personnel. This is where cloud computing emerged as a game-changer, offering financial institutions a more flexible, scalable, and cost-effective solution to their data management needs.

The adoption of cloud computing in finance initially began with non-core functions such as customer relationship management (CRM), human resources, and payroll systems. However, as cloud technology matured and proved its reliability, financial institutions started to explore its potential in core operations such as risk management, trading, and financial reporting.

Today, cloud financial operations have become an integral part of the financial industry, with institutions leveraging the power of cloud computing to streamline processes, enhance data security, and drive innovation. Major players in the financial sector, including banks, insurance companies, and investment firms, have embraced cloud technology to varying degrees, with some even adopting a cloud-first strategy.

The rise of cloud computing in finance has also given birth to an entirely new ecosystem of FinTech startups and technology providers, offering specialized cloud-based solutions tailored to the unique needs of financial institutions. This has further fueled the growth and adoption of cloud financial operations, as organizations have access to a wide array of tools and services designed specifically for their industry.

In summary, the roots of cloud computing in finance can be traced back to the early days of time-sharing and the internet, but its true potential has only been realized in recent years. As financial institutions continue to embrace cloud technology and its myriad benefits, the future of cloud financial operations looks brighter than ever.

Empowering Financial Professionals in the Cloud Age

The primary purpose of this book is to empower financial professionals by providing them with the knowledge, tools, and strategies necessary to thrive in the rapidly evolving world of cloud financial operations. As the digital revolution transforms the financial industry, professionals must stay ahead of the curve and adapt to the new landscape. This book aims to serve as a comprehensive guide for those who are ready to embrace the cloud and harness its potential to drive financial success.

In the Cloud Age, financial professionals are no longer confined to the traditional boundaries of brick-and-mortar offices and cumbersome, outdated systems. Instead, they can now access, analyze, and manage financial data from anywhere in the world, at any time, thanks to the power of cloud computing. This unprecedented level of **flexibility and efficiency** has opened up a world of possibilities for businesses and individuals alike, enabling them to make more informed decisions, streamline their operations, and ultimately achieve greater financial success.

However, with great power comes great responsibility. As financial professionals navigate the uncharted waters of cloud financial operations, they must also be prepared to face new challenges and risks, such as data security, regulatory compliance, and the ever-changing landscape of cloud-based technologies. This book aims to equip readers with the necessary knowledge and skills to overcome these obstacles and make the most of the opportunities presented by the cloud.

By delving into topics such as the history of cloud computing in finance, the various cloud-based financial tools and platforms available, and best practices for implementing and managing cloud financial operations, this book provides readers with a solid foundation upon which they can build their own cloud-driven financial success stories. Furthermore, the author's unique perspective as an industry expert offers valuable insights and practical advice that can only be gained through years of experience in the field.

In conclusion, this book aims to empower financial professionals to navigate the complexities of cloud financial operations with confidence and ease. By providing a comprehensive guide to the world of cloud finance, this book aims to help readers unlock the full potential of the cloud and propel their careers and businesses to new heights in the Cloud Age.

Navigating the Complexities of Cloud Financial Operations

In today's rapidly evolving financial landscape, the adoption of cloud computing has become a game-changer for organizations of all sizes. As we delve into the world of cloud financial operations, this book aims to provide a comprehensive and insightful guide to help you navigate the complexities and challenges of this new era of finance.

The scope of this book is broad yet focused, covering various aspects of cloud financial operations, including the following:

Understanding the fundamentals: We will start by exploring the basic concepts and principles of cloud computing and how they apply to the financial industry. This will lay the groundwork for a deeper understanding of the advantages and challenges that cloud-based financial systems present.

Cloud financial management tools and platforms: A key component of successful cloud financial operations is the effective use of tools and platforms designed specifically for this purpose. We will examine the various options available, their features, and how to choose the right one for your organization.

Compliance and security: As financial data is highly sensitive and subject to stringent regulations, ensuring compliance and maintaining security in the cloud is of utmost importance. This book will provide guidance on how to address these concerns and implement best practices to safeguard your organization's financial data.

Cost management and optimization: One of the primary drivers for adopting cloud computing is the potential for cost savings. We will explore strategies for effective cost management and optimization in cloud financial operations, ensuring that your organization reaps the full benefits of this technology.

Integration and automation: Integrating cloud financial operations with other systems and automating tasks is essential to maximize efficiency and streamline processes. We will discuss the various approaches to integration and automation, and how they can be leveraged to improve your organization's financial performance.

Future trends and innovations: As the cloud continues to evolve, so will the world of financial operations. This book will touch upon emerging trends and innovations in cloud computing that are set to shape the future of finance, preparing you to stay ahead of the curve.

By covering these topics, this book aims to equip financial professionals with the knowledge and tools necessary to successfully navigate the complexities of cloud financial operations. Through real-world examples, practical advice, and expert insights, you will thoroughly understand the cloud's impact on finance and how to harness its potential for your organization's success.

Insights from an Industry Expert

As an author and industry expert, I have witnessed the rapid evolution of cloud computing in the financial sector. Over the years, I have worked closely with various organizations, helping them transition from traditional financial operations to cloud-based systems. This journey has given me invaluable insights into the challenges, opportunities, and best practices associated with cloud financial operations.

One of the most significant insights I have gained is the importance of embracing change. The financial industry, historically known for its conservative approach, has been somewhat slow to adopt new technologies. However, the advent of cloud computing has disrupted traditional financial operations, necessitating a more agile and forward-thinking mindset. Financial professionals must be willing to adapt and evolve, as clinging to outdated systems and processes will only hinder their growth and success in the long run.

Another key insight is the need for a strong foundation in both **finance and technology.** Cloud financial operations require a unique blend of skills and knowledge, as professionals must understand the intricacies of financial management and navigate the complexities of cloud computing. This dual expertise is essential for making informed decisions, optimizing processes, and ensuring the security and compliance of financial data in the cloud.

Collaboration and communication are also critical in the realm of cloud financial operations. As organizations increasingly adopt cloud-based systems, financial professionals must work closely with IT teams, vendors, and other stakeholders to ensure seamless integration and efficient workflows. This requires a willingness to listen, learn, and adapt and the ability to articulate complex financial concepts and requirements in a way that resonates with diverse audiences.

Lastly, I have learned the importance of staying informed and up-to-date on industry trends and developments. The cloud computing landscape is constantly evolving, with new tools, technologies, and best practices emerging rapidly. Financial professionals must commit to ongoing education and professional development, as this will enable them to stay ahead of the curve and harness the full potential of cloud financial operations.

In conclusion, my experience as an industry expert has taught me that success in cloud financial operations hinges on adaptability, collaboration, and continuous learning. By embracing these principles and leveraging the insights shared in this book, financial professionals can confidently navigate the complexities of the cloud and unlock new levels of efficiency, innovation, and growth.

Setting the Stage for Cloud-Driven Financial Success

As we stand on the precipice of a new financial era, it is clear that cloud financial operations are no longer a futuristic concept but rather an essential component of modern business practices. The rapid evolution of technology and the increasing need for real-time, data-driven decision-making have propelled cloud computing to the forefront of the financial industry. By embracing this paradigm shift, financial professionals can unlock unprecedented opportunities for growth, efficiency, and innovation.

In this book, we have embarked on a journey to explore the intricacies of cloud financial operations, delving into its origins, applications, and best practices. **Our goal has been to empower you,** the financial professional, with the knowledge and tools necessary to navigate this complex landscape with confidence and skill. By understanding the nuances of cloud computing in finance, you can harness its full potential and drive your organization toward unparalleled success.

As an industry expert, I have witnessed firsthand the transformative power of cloud financial operations. The insights and experiences shared in this book testify to the immense value cloud computing can bring to the financial sector. By leveraging the agility, scalability, and cost-effectiveness of cloud-based solutions, financial professionals can revolutionize their organizations and redefine the way they approach their work.

In conclusion, the future of finance is undoubtedly intertwined with the cloud. As we move forward, it is crucial for financial professionals to embrace this new reality and adapt to the ever-changing landscape of cloud financial operations. By doing so, we can set the stage for a future of cloud-driven financial success, where innovation, efficiency, and growth become the hallmarks of our industry.

So, let us embark on this exciting journey together as we explore the limitless possibilities that cloud financial operations have to offer. The future is bright, and the sky is truly the limit.

THE EVOLUTION OF CLOUD COMPUTING IN FINANCE

A futuristic cityscape where buildings are connected by beams of light, symbolizing cloud computing networks.

I n the ever-evolving world of finance, the need for innovative solutions to manage data, improve operational efficiency, and enhance customer experiences has become increasingly critical. Financial institutions are constantly seeking ways to stay ahead of the curve as the industry continues to face mounting challenges, such as stringent regulatory requirements, heightened competition, and the growing demand for real-time data analysis. One such revolutionary development that has transformed the landscape of finance is the advent of cloud computing.

Cloud computing, a technology that allows users to access and store data, applications, and resources over the internet, has emerged as a game-changer in the finance industry. This paradigm shift from traditional, on-premise financial systems to cloud-based solutions has enabled organizations to streamline their operations and explore new avenues for growth and innovation.

The emergence of cloud computing in finance can be traced back to the early 2000s when the concept of **Software as a Service (SaaS)** began to gain traction. SaaS, a cloud computing model that allows users to access software applications over the internet, provided financial institutions with a more cost-effective and scalable alternative to traditional software installations. As the benefits of SaaS became increasingly apparent, the adoption of cloud computing in finance began to accelerate.

Over the past decade, the finance industry has witnessed a rapid expansion in cloud computing, with organizations of all sizes embracing this transformative technology. From small and medium-sized enterprises (SMEs) to large multinational corporations, financial institutions have recognized the immense potential of cloud computing to enhance their operational efficiency, reduce costs, and drive innovation.

In this chapter, we will delve deeper into the evolution of cloud computing in finance, exploring the factors that have contributed to its widespread adoption and examining the impact of this technology on the industry as a whole. Through a series of case studies, we will also highlight the successes and challenges financial institutions face in implementing cloud-based solutions, providing valuable insights into the future of cloud computing in finance and beyond.

The Shift from Traditional Financial Systems to Cloud-Based Solutions

The finance industry has always been at the forefront of technological advancements, and the adoption of cloud computing is no exception. In recent years, there has been a significant shift from traditional financial systems to cloud-based solutions, driven by the need for increased efficiency, cost reduction, and improved scalability. This section will explore the factors that have contributed to this shift and the benefits cloud computing brings to the finance industry.

One of the primary reasons for the shift towards cloud-based solutions in finance is the **need for greater efficiency**. Traditional financial systems often involve complex, time-consuming processes that can be prone to errors. On the other hand, cloud computing offers a more streamlined approach, with automated processes and real-time data access that can significantly reduce the time and effort required to complete tasks. This increased efficiency not only saves time but also helps to reduce the risk of costly errors, making it an attractive option for finance professionals.

Another key factor driving the shift towards cloud-based solutions is the **potential for cost reduction**. Traditional financial systems often require significant upfront investments in hardware and software, as well as ongoing maintenance and upgrade costs. However, cloud computing operates on a pay-as-you-go model, allowing businesses to only pay for the resources they use. This can lead to significant cost savings, particularly for smaller businesses and startups that may not have the capital to invest in expensive infrastructure.

Scalability is another important consideration for finance professionals when evaluating the benefits of cloud computing. Traditional financial systems can be difficult and costly to scale, often requiring additional hardware and software investments to accommodate growth.

Cloud-based solutions, however, are designed to be easily scalable, allowing businesses to quickly and easily adjust their resources as needed. This flexibility is particularly valuable in the fast-paced world of finance, where businesses must be able to adapt to changing market conditions and customer demands.

The shift towards cloud-based solutions in finance has also been fueled by the increasing **need for improved data security and compliance**. Financial institutions are subject to strict data protection and privacy regulations, and cloud computing providers have responded by offering robust security measures and compliance tools. This has helped to alleviate concerns about the safety of sensitive financial data, making cloud-based solutions an increasingly attractive option for businesses in the finance industry.

In conclusion, the shift from traditional financial systems to cloud-based solutions has been driven by a combination of factors, including the need for increased efficiency, cost reduction, scalability, and improved data security. As more and more businesses in the finance industry recognize the benefits of cloud computing, this trend will likely continue to gain momentum, shaping the future of financial operations and services.

Key Drivers of Cloud Adoption in the Finance Industry

The rapid adoption of cloud computing in the finance industry can be attributed to several key drivers that have made it an attractive and viable option for businesses of all sizes. In this section, we will explore the most significant factors that have contributed to the widespread acceptance and implementation of cloud-based solutions in the finance sector.

Cost Efficiency: One of the primary drivers of cloud adoption in finance is the potential for significant cost savings. Traditional financial systems often require substantial investments in hardware, software, and IT infrastructure, as well as ongoing maintenance and support costs. Cloud-based solutions, on the other hand, operate on a pay-as-you-go model, allowing businesses to scale their usage and expenses according to their needs. This eliminates the need for large upfront investments and reduces the total cost of ownership.

Scalability and Flexibility: Cloud computing offers unparalleled scalability and flexibility, enabling financial institutions to easily adjust their computing resources based on demand. This is particularly beneficial for businesses experiencing rapid growth or seasonal fluctuations, as they can quickly scale up or down without needing additional hardware or infrastructure investments. This level of agility is essential in today's fast-paced and ever-changing financial landscape.

Enhanced Security and Compliance: Security and regulatory compliance are top priorities for financial institutions, and cloud providers have significantly addressed these concerns. Many cloud-based solutions now offer advanced security features, such as encryption, multi-factor authentication, and intrusion detection systems, to protect sensitive financial data. Additionally, cloud providers often undergo rigorous audits to ensure compliance with industry-specific regulations, such as the Payment Card Industry Data Security Standard (PCI DSS) and the General Data Protection Regulation (GDPR).

Improved Collaboration and Accessibility: Cloud-based financial systems enable seamless collaboration and data sharing among team members, regardless of their physical location. This is particularly valuable for organizations with multiple offices or remote employees, as it allows for real-time access to financial data and streamlined communication. Furthermore, cloud solutions often include mobile applications, enabling users to access critical financial information from any device at any time.

Integration and Automation: Cloud computing facilitates seamless integration with other software applications and tools, streamlining financial processes and reducing manual tasks. This allows financial professionals to focus on more strategic and value-added activities, such as data analysis and decision-making. Moreover, cloud-based solutions often include built-in automation features, such as automated invoicing and expense tracking, further improving efficiency and accuracy.

Innovation and Competitive Advantage: Adopting cloud-based financial solutions enables businesses to stay ahead of the curve by leveraging the latest technologies and innovations. Cloud providers continuously update and improve their offerings, ensuring that users have access to cutting-edge tools and features. This enhances the overall user experience and provides a competitive advantage in an increasingly digital and data-driven financial landscape.

In conclusion, the key drivers of cloud adoption in the finance industry are numerous and compelling. From cost efficiency and scalability to enhanced security and compliance, cloud-based solutions offer a myriad of benefits that have made them an essential component of modern financial operations. As the industry continues to evolve and embrace digital transformation, the adoption of cloud computing is poised to play an even more significant role in shaping the future of finance.

The Impact of Cloud Computing on Financial Services and Operations

The advent of cloud computing has brought about a paradigm shift in the way financial services and operations are conducted. As more and more organizations embrace this technology, the impact on the finance industry has been nothing short of transformative. In this section, we will delve into the various ways cloud computing has revolutionized financial services and operations, leading to increased efficiency, cost savings, and enhanced security.

One of the most significant impacts of cloud computing on financial services is the increased **accessibility to data and applications**. With cloud-based solutions, financial institutions can now access their data and applications from anywhere, at any time, and on any device. This has improved the efficiency of financial operations and enabled organizations to provide better customer service by offering real-time access to account information and transactions.

Another notable impact of cloud computing on financial services is the **reduction in operational costs**. Traditional financial systems often require significant investments in hardware, software, and IT infrastructure, which can be a burden for organizations, especially smaller ones. Cloud-based solutions, on the other hand, operate on a pay-as-you-go model, allowing organizations to scale their resources according to their needs and budget. This has led to substantial cost savings for financial institutions, as they no longer need to maintain expensive on-premise infrastructure.

In addition to cost savings, cloud computing has also enabled financial institutions to streamline their operations and **improve overall efficiency**. With cloud-based solutions, organizations can automate repetitive tasks like data entry and report generation, freeing up valuable time and resources for more strategic initiatives. Furthermore, the ability to integrate various financial applications and tools through APIs (Application Programming Interfaces) has facilitated seamless data flow between systems, leading to better decision-making and reduced errors.

Security is a top concern for financial institutions, and cloud computing has significantly impacted how organizations approach data protection. Cloud service providers invest heavily in state-of-the-art security measures, such as encryption, multi-factor authentication, and regular security audits, to ensure the safety of their clients' data. By leveraging these advanced security features, financial institutions can safeguard sensitive information and maintain compliance with industry regulations.

Lastly, cloud computing has fostered innovation in the finance industry by providing a platform for developing and deploying new financial products and services. Fintech startups, in particular, have leveraged cloud technology to disrupt traditional financial services, offering innovative solutions such as mobile banking, peer-to-peer lending, and digital wallets. These new offerings have provided customers with more convenient and personalized financial services and pushed established financial institutions to innovate and adapt to the changing landscape.

In conclusion, the impact of cloud computing on financial services and operations has been profound and far-reaching. From increased accessibility and cost savings to enhanced security and innovation, cloud technology has transformed the way financial institutions conduct business and serve their customers. As cloud adoption continues to grow, we can expect even more significant advancements and innovations in the finance industry, shaping the future of financial services for years to come.

Case Studies: Successful Cloud Implementation in Finance

This section will explore some real-life examples of successful cloud implementation in the finance industry. These case studies will demonstrate how cloud computing has transformed financial operations, improved efficiency, and enabled organizations to stay ahead in an increasingly competitive landscape.

Case Study 1: Bank of America

Bank of America, one of the largest financial institutions in the world, has embraced cloud computing to streamline its operations and enhance customer experience. The bank adopted a hybrid cloud strategy combining private and public cloud solutions to optimize its IT infrastructure and reduce costs.

By leveraging cloud technology, Bank of America was able to consolidate its data centers, resulting in significant cost savings. Additionally, the bank's move to the cloud enabled it to scale its operations and services rapidly, meeting the growing demands of its customers. The cloud also allowed the bank to deploy new applications and services faster, improving its agility and competitiveness in the market.

Case Study 2: Xero

Xero, a leading cloud-based accounting software provider, has revolutionized the way small businesses manage their finances. By offering a comprehensive suite of financial tools and services on the cloud, Xero has made it easier for businesses to access their financial data anytime, anywhere, and on any device.

Xero's cloud-based platform has enabled it to deliver real-time financial data to its users, allowing them to make informed decisions and manage their cash flow more effectively. The platform's seamless integration with other cloud-based applications has also helped businesses automate various financial processes, saving time and resources.

Case Study 3: PayPal

PayPal, a global leader in online payments, has leveraged cloud computing to scale its operations and support its rapid growth. By migrating its data centers to the cloud, PayPal has been able to process billions of transactions securely and efficiently, serving millions of customers worldwide.

The cloud has also allowed PayPal to innovate and introduce new features and services at a faster pace, enhancing its product offerings and staying ahead of the competition. Moreover, the company's use of cloud technology has enabled it to maintain high levels of security and compliance, ensuring the protection of sensitive financial data.

In conclusion, these case studies demonstrate the transformative power of cloud computing in the finance industry. By adopting cloud-based solutions, financial institutions and service providers have optimized their operations, reduced costs, and delivered better customer service. As cloud technology continues to evolve, we can expect to see even more innovative applications and use cases in the finance sector, driving further growth and success.

The Future of Cloud Computing in Finance and Beyond

In conclusion, the rapid evolution of cloud computing in the finance industry has transformed the way organizations manage their financial operations. The shift from traditional financial systems to cloud-based solutions has been driven by the need for increased efficiency, cost reduction, and improved scalability. As we have seen, cloud computing has profoundly impacted financial services and operations, enabling businesses to streamline processes, enhance collaboration, and make data-driven decisions.

Looking ahead, the future of cloud computing in finance is even more promising. As technology continues to advance, we can expect to see further innovations in cloud-based financial solutions that will continue to revolutionize the industry. Here are some key trends and developments that are likely to shape the future of cloud computing in finance:

Artificial Intelligence (AI) and Machine Learning (ML): The integration of AI and ML capabilities into cloud-based financial systems will enable organizations to automate complex tasks, analyze vast amounts of data, and make more accurate predictions. This will improve efficiency and help businesses identify new opportunities and mitigate risks more effectively.

Blockchain Technology: The adoption of blockchain technology in cloud-based financial solutions will enhance the security, transparency, and traceability of transactions. This will be particularly beneficial for industries such as banking and insurance, where trust and data integrity are of utmost importance.

Advanced Analytics and Big Data: As the volume of financial data continues to grow, advanced analytics and big data capabilities will become increasingly important for organizations to gain valuable insights and make informed decisions. Cloud-based financial systems will be equipped with sophisticated tools to process and analyze large datasets, enabling businesses to identify trends, patterns, and correlations that were previously hidden.

Enhanced Integration and Interoperability: The future of cloud computing in finance will see greater integration and interoperability between different financial systems and applications. This will allow organizations to seamlessly share data and collaborate across various platforms, leading to improved efficiency and better decision-making.

Increased Regulatory Compliance: As financial regulations continue to evolve, cloud-based financial systems will be designed to ensure that organizations remain compliant with the latest rules and standards. This will help businesses avoid costly penalties and enhance their reputation and credibility in the market.

Greater Focus on Cybersecurity: As the reliance on cloud-based financial solutions grows, so will the need for robust cybersecurity measures to protect sensitive data and systems from potential threats. The future of cloud computing in finance will see the development of advanced security features and protocols to safeguard businesses against cyberattacks and data breaches.

In summary, the future of cloud computing in finance is bright, with numerous opportunities for innovation and growth. As businesses continue to embrace cloud-based solutions, we can expect to see a more efficient, secure, and data-driven financial landscape that will benefit organizations and consumers alike. The journey toward a fully cloud-enabled finance industry has only just begun, and it is an exciting time to be part of this transformation.

Chapter Summary

- Cloud computing has emerged as a game-changer in the finance industry, enabling organizations to streamline operations, reduce costs, and drive innovation.
- The shift from traditional financial systems to cloud-based solutions has been driven by the need for increased efficiency, cost reduction, scalability, and improved data security.
- Key drivers of cloud adoption in finance include cost efficiency, scalability and flexibility, enhanced security and compliance, improved collaboration and accessibility, integration and automation, and innovation and competitive advantage.
- Cloud computing has revolutionized financial services and operations by increasing accessibility to data and applications, reducing operational costs, streamlining processes, enhancing security, and fostering innovation.

- Successful cloud implementation in finance can be seen in case studies of Bank of America, Xero, and PayPal, demonstrating the transformative power of cloud computing in the industry.
- The future of cloud computing in finance will be shaped by trends such as artificial intelligence and machine learning, blockchain technology, advanced analytics and big data, enhanced integration and interoperability, increased regulatory compliance, and a greater focus on cybersecurity.
- Cloud-based financial systems will continue to evolve, offering sophisticated tools for data processing and analysis, seamless integration with other platforms, and advanced security features to protect sensitive information.
- The ongoing adoption of cloud computing in finance will lead to a more efficient, secure, and data-driven financial landscape, benefiting organizations and consumers alike.

2

KEY COMPONENTS OF CLOUD
FINANCIAL OPERATIONS

An image illustrating the seamless integration of cloud-based financial systems with various devices.

In today's rapidly evolving digital landscape, businesses are increasingly turning to cloud-based solutions to streamline their operations, improve efficiency, and reduce costs. As organizations continue to migrate their workloads and applications to the cloud, it becomes crucial to have a robust financial strategy in place to manage and optimize the costs associated with cloud services. This is where **cloud financial operations** come into play.

Cloud financial operations, often referred to as FinOps, is the practice of managing and optimizing the financial aspects of cloud computing. It involves a combination of tools, processes, and best practices that enable organizations to gain visibility into their cloud spending, allocate resources efficiently, and ensure they get the most value out of their cloud investments. By implementing a strong cloud financial operations strategy, businesses can effectively control their cloud costs, drive innovation, and achieve a competitive advantage in the market.

In this chapter, we will explore the key components of cloud financial operations, which include cost management and optimization, financial governance and compliance, cloud budgeting and forecasting, and performance monitoring and reporting. By understanding these critical elements, you will be well-equipped to build a successful cloud financial strategy that aligns with your organization's goals and objectives.

As we delve into the world of cloud financial operations, it is essential to recognize that this is not a one-size-fits-all approach. Each organization's cloud journey is unique, and its challenges and opportunities will vary. However, by adopting a proactive and strategic approach to managing your cloud finances, you can ensure that your organization is well-positioned to capitalize on the benefits of cloud computing while minimizing the risks associated with cloud costs.

In the following sections, we will provide you with the knowledge and insights needed to navigate the complexities of cloud financial operations and develop a comprehensive strategy that drives value for your organization. So, let's embark on this exciting journey together and unlock the full potential of your cloud investments.

Cost Management and Optimization

In today's rapidly evolving digital landscape, businesses are increasingly turning to cloud-based solutions to streamline their operations and drive growth. As organizations migrate their infrastructure and applications to the cloud, effective cost management and optimization become critical components of a successful cloud financial strategy. In this section, we will explore the key aspects of cost management and optimization in cloud financial operations and discuss the best practices for achieving maximum value from your cloud investments.

First, it is essential to understand that cost management in the cloud is a continuous process rather than a one-time exercise. As your organization's cloud usage expands and evolves, so will the associated costs and potential savings opportunities. Therefore, it is crucial to establish a proactive approach to cost management that encompasses regular monitoring, analysis, and optimization efforts.

One of the primary drivers of cloud cost optimization is the **efficient utilization of resources.** Cloud providers offer a wide range of services and pricing models, which can be tailored to meet your organization's specific needs. By carefully selecting the right mix of services and resource configurations, you can significantly reduce your cloud expenses while maintaining optimal performance. Some key strategies for resource optimization include:

- **Right-sizing:** Ensure that your cloud resources are appropriately sized to match your workload requirements. Regularly review and adjust resource allocations to avoid over-provisioning or under-utilizing resources.
- **Auto-scaling:** Implement auto-scaling policies to dynamically adjust resource capacity based on real-time demand. This can help you maintain optimal performance during peak periods while minimizing costs during periods of low demand.
- **Reserved instances and savings plans:** Take advantage of discounted pricing options offered by cloud providers for

long-term commitments. By reserving instances or committing to a savings plan, you can secure significant cost savings compared to on-demand pricing.

In addition to resource optimization, effective cost management also involves closely **monitoring and controlling your cloud expenses.** This can be achieved by implementing financial governance policies and using cloud cost management tools. Some key aspects of financial governance include:

- **Budgeting and cost allocation:** Establish clear budgets for your cloud projects and allocate costs to specific departments or business units. This will help you maintain visibility and control over your cloud expenses and ensure that costs are accurately attributed to the relevant stakeholders.
- **Cost monitoring and alerting:** Regularly monitor your cloud expenses and set up alerts to notify you of any unexpected cost increases or anomalies. This will enable you to quickly identify and address potential issues before they escalate.
- **Cost optimization recommendations:** Leverage cloud provider tools and third-party solutions to generate cost optimization recommendations. These tools can help you identify opportunities for savings, such as unused resources, under-utilized instances, or more cost-effective service options.

In conclusion, effective cost management and optimization are essential components of a successful cloud financial strategy. By adopting a proactive approach to resource utilization, financial governance, and continuous monitoring, your organization can maximize the value of its cloud investments and drive long-term growth. In the next section, we will delve deeper into the topic of financial governance and compliance in cloud financial operations.

Financial Governance and Compliance

This section will delve into the crucial aspect of financial governance and compliance in cloud financial operations. As organizations increasingly adopt cloud services, it is essential to establish a robust framework that ensures the efficient management of financial resources while adhering to industry standards and regulations. By the end of this section, you will have a comprehensive understanding of the key components of financial governance and compliance, and how they contribute to the overall success of your cloud financial strategy.

Financial governance refers to the set of policies, processes, and controls that guide an organization's financial decision-making and resource allocation. In the context of cloud financial operations, financial governance encompasses the management of cloud costs, risk mitigation, and adherence to regulatory requirements. Implementing effective financial governance practices is vital to ensure your organization's cloud investments align with its strategic objectives and deliver optimal value.

Compliance, on the other hand, refers to the adherence to industry standards, regulations, and best practices that govern the use of cloud services. Compliance is a critical aspect of financial governance, as it ensures that your organization's cloud operations meet the necessary legal and regulatory requirements, thereby mitigating the risk of penalties, fines, and reputational damage.

Let's explore the key components of financial governance and compliance in cloud financial operations:

Cost Management Policies: Establishing clear policies for cloud cost management is the foundation of effective financial governance. These policies should define the roles and responsibilities of various stakeholders, set guidelines for cloud resource usage, and outline the processes for monitoring and controlling costs. By implementing cost management policies, organizations can prevent overspending, optimize resource utilization, and ensure that cloud investments are aligned with business goals.

Risk Management: Cloud financial operations involve inherent risks, such as fluctuating costs, data breaches, and service outages. A robust financial governance framework should include risk management strategies to identify, assess, and mitigate these risks. This may involve conducting regular risk assessments, implementing security measures, and establishing contingency plans to minimize the impact of unforeseen events on your organization's cloud operations.

Compliance Monitoring: Ensuring compliance with industry standards and regulations is a critical aspect of financial governance. Organizations should implement processes to continuously monitor their cloud operations for compliance with relevant laws, such as data protection regulations and industry-specific requirements. This may involve conducting regular audits, implementing automated compliance checks, and maintaining up-to-date documentation of your organization's cloud compliance efforts.

Training and Awareness: Effective financial governance and compliance require the active involvement of all stakeholders, from executive leadership to individual employees. Organizations should invest in training and awareness programs to ensure all team members understand their roles and responsibilities in managing cloud costs and maintaining compliance. This will help create a culture of accountability and foster a proactive approach to cloud financial management.

Continuous Improvement: Financial governance and compliance are not static processes; they must evolve as your organization's cloud operations grow and change. Regularly reviewing and updating your financial governance framework will help ensure it remains effective in managing costs, mitigating risks, and maintaining compliance. This may involve incorporating new best practices, refining existing policies, and adopting new tools and technologies to enhance your organization's cloud financial operations.

In conclusion, financial governance and compliance are critical components of a successful cloud financial strategy. By implementing robust policies, processes, and controls, organizations can effectively manage their cloud costs, mitigate risks, and ensure adherence to industry standards and regulations. As your organization continues to embrace cloud services, a strong focus on financial governance and compliance will be essential to maximize the value of your cloud investments and drive long-term success.

Cloud Budgeting and Forecasting

In today's fast-paced and ever-evolving digital landscape, organizations are increasingly turning to cloud-based solutions to streamline their financial operations. As a result, cloud budgeting and forecasting have emerged as critical components of a successful cloud financial strategy. This section will delve into the importance of cloud budgeting and forecasting, explore best practices, and discuss how to effectively implement these processes within your organization.

Cloud budgeting and forecasting are essential for organizations to effectively manage their cloud expenses, allocate resources, and plan for future growth. By accurately predicting and monitoring cloud costs, organizations can make informed decisions, optimize their cloud investments, and avoid unexpected expenses.

First, it is crucial to understand the difference between cloud budgeting and forecasting. **Cloud budgeting** involves setting financial targets and allocating resources for a specific period, typically on an annual basis. This process helps organizations establish a clear roadmap for their cloud expenses and ensures they stay within their financial limits. On the other hand, cloud **forecasting** is the process of predicting future cloud costs based on historical data, current trends, and anticipated changes in the cloud environment. Forecasting allows organizations to anticipate fluctuations in cloud usage and adjust their budgets accordingly.Here are some best practices for effective cloud budgeting and forecasting:

Establish clear goals and objectives: Before embarking on the cloud budgeting and forecasting process, it is essential to define your organization's goals and objectives. This will help you align your cloud financial strategy with your overall business strategy and ensure that your cloud investments are driving value for your organization.

Leverage historical data and trends: Analyzing historical data and identifying trends in your cloud usage can provide valuable insights for your budgeting and forecasting efforts. By understanding how your organization has utilized cloud resources in the past, you can better predict future usage patterns and allocate resources accordingly.

Implement a robust cloud cost management tool: Utilizing a cloud cost management tool can greatly simplify the budgeting and forecasting process. These tools can help you track and analyze your cloud expenses, identify cost-saving opportunities, and generate accurate forecasts based on real-time data.

Involve stakeholders from across the organization: Cloud budgeting and forecasting should not be the sole responsibility of the finance team. Instead, involve stakeholders from various departments, such as IT, operations, and business units, to ensure that your cloud financial strategy aligns with the needs and priorities of the entire organization.

Monitor and adjust your budget and forecast regularly: Cloud environments are dynamic, and your organization's cloud usage patterns may change over time. Regularly reviewing and adjusting your cloud budget and forecast can help you stay on top of these changes and ensure that your cloud financial strategy remains relevant and effective.

momalein **Plan for contingencies:** Unexpected events, such as sudden spikes in cloud usage or changes in cloud pricing, can significantly impact your cloud expenses. Incorporating contingencies into your cloud budget and forecast can help you prepare for these uncertainties and ensure that your organization can adapt to changes in the cloud environment.

In conclusion, cloud budgeting and forecasting are essential components of a successful cloud financial strategy. By implementing these processes effectively, organizations can optimize their cloud investments, manage their cloud expenses, and drive value from their cloud initiatives. As the cloud continues to transform the way organizations operate, mastering cloud budgeting and forecasting will be critical to staying competitive in the digital age.

Performance Monitoring and Reporting

In today's fast-paced and competitive business environment, organizations need to have a clear understanding of their cloud financial operations' performance. Performance monitoring and reporting are crucial in ensuring that organizations can make informed decisions and optimize their cloud investments. This section will discuss the importance of performance monitoring and reporting, the key metrics to track, and best practices for effective reporting.

The primary goal of performance monitoring and reporting is to provide organizations with actionable insights into their cloud financial operations. This enables them to identify areas of improvement, optimize costs, and ensure that their cloud investments are aligned with their strategic goals. By regularly monitoring and reporting on key performance indicators (KPIs), organizations can quickly identify trends, detect anomalies, and take corrective actions to maintain optimal performance.

Some of the key metrics that organizations should track as part of their performance monitoring and reporting efforts include:

- **Cost per workload:** This metric helps organizations understand the cost of running each workload in the cloud. By tracking this metric, organizations can identify workloads that are more expensive than expected and take steps to optimize their costs.
- **Resource utilization:** This metric measures resource usage efficiency in the cloud. High resource utilization indicates that an organization effectively uses its cloud resources, while low resource utilization may suggest that resources are being wasted or underutilized.
- **Cost savings:** This metric tracks the cost savings achieved through various cost optimization efforts, such as right-sizing, reserved instances, and spot instances. By monitoring this metric, organizations can quantify the impact of their

cost optimization initiatives and identify areas where further savings can be achieved.

- **Budget variance:** This metric compares actual cloud spending against the budgeted amount. A positive variance indicates that an organization is spending less than its budget, while a negative variance suggests overspending. Monitoring budget variance helps organizations maintain financial control and make necessary adjustments to their cloud financial strategy.

To ensure effective performance monitoring and reporting, organizations should follow these best practices:

- **Establish clear KPIs:** Organizations should define clear and measurable KPIs that align with their strategic goals. This will ensure that their performance monitoring and reporting efforts are focused on the most critical aspects of their cloud financial operations.
- **Automate data collection and reporting:** Organizations should leverage cloud-native tools and third-party solutions to automate data collection and reporting. This will help them save time and resources while ensuring their reports are accurate and up-to-date.
- **Customize reports for different stakeholders:** Different stakeholders within an organization may have different information needs. Therefore, organizations should customize their reports to cater to the specific needs of each stakeholder group, ensuring that they receive relevant and actionable insights.
- **Regularly review and update KPIs:** As organizations evolve and their cloud financial operations mature, their KPIs may need to be updated to reflect new priorities and goals. Regularly reviewing and updating KPIs will ensure that performance monitoring and reporting efforts remain relevant and effective.

In conclusion, performance monitoring and reporting are essential components of a successful cloud financial strategy. By tracking key metrics and following best practices, organizations can gain valuable insights into their cloud financial operations, optimize costs, and ensure that their cloud investments are aligned with their strategic goals.

Building a Successful Cloud Financial Strategy

In today's rapidly evolving digital landscape, cloud financial operations have become an essential aspect of business success. As organizations continue to migrate their operations to the cloud, it is crucial to develop and implement a robust cloud financial strategy that encompasses all key components discussed in this chapter. By doing so, businesses can effectively manage costs, ensure compliance, and make informed decisions that drive growth and innovation.

To build a successful cloud financial strategy, organizations must first establish a strong foundation by understanding the unique characteristics and challenges of cloud financial operations. This includes recognizing the dynamic nature of cloud costs, the need for real-time visibility into financial data, and the importance of **collaboration** between IT and finance teams.

Next, organizations must prioritize **cost management and optimization**. By leveraging tools and techniques such as right-sizing, reserved instances, and spot instances, businesses can significantly reduce their cloud expenses without compromising performance or scalability. Additionally, organizations should establish a culture of cost awareness and accountability, encouraging employees to consider the financial implications of their actions in the cloud.

Financial governance and compliance are also critical components of a successful cloud financial strategy. By implementing policies, processes, and controls, organizations can minimize risks associated with regulatory non-compliance, data breaches, and other security threats. This includes establishing clear roles and responsibilities, enforcing data protection measures, and conducting regular audits to ensure ongoing compliance.

Cloud budgeting and forecasting are crucial in maintaining financial stability and driving strategic decision-making. By developing accurate, data-driven budgets and forecasts, organizations can allocate resources more effectively, identify potential cost savings, and anticipate future financial needs. This requires a deep understanding of historical trends and the ability to adapt to changing market conditions and business requirements.

Performance monitoring and reporting are essential for tracking the success of a cloud financial strategy and identifying areas for improvement. By establishing **key performance indicators (KPIs)** and leveraging advanced analytics tools, organizations can gain valuable insights into their cloud spending patterns, resource utilization, and overall financial performance. This information can then be used to inform future decision-making and drive continuous improvement.

In conclusion, building a successful cloud financial strategy requires a comprehensive approach that addresses all key components of cloud financial operations. By focusing on cost management, financial governance, budgeting, forecasting, and performance monitoring, organizations can effectively navigate the complexities of the cloud and unlock its full potential for growth and innovation. As the cloud continues to evolve, businesses that embrace these best practices will be well-positioned to thrive in the competitive digital landscape.

Chapter Summary

- Cloud financial operations, or FinOps, is essential for managing and optimizing the financial aspects of cloud computing, helping organizations control costs, drive innovation, and gain a competitive advantage.
- Effective cost management and optimization involve continuous monitoring, analysis, and optimization efforts,

including right-sizing, auto-scaling, and leveraging reserved instances and savings plans.

- Financial governance and compliance are critical components of a successful cloud financial strategy, ensuring efficient management of financial resources and adherence to industry standards and regulations.
- Cloud budgeting and forecasting are essential for managing cloud expenses, allocating resources, and planning for future growth, requiring a deep understanding of historical trends and the ability to adapt to changing market conditions.
- Performance monitoring and reporting provide organizations with actionable insights into their cloud financial operations, enabling them to identify areas of improvement, optimize costs, and ensure alignment with strategic goals.
- Establishing clear KPIs, automating data collection and reporting, and customizing reports for different stakeholders are best practices for effective performance monitoring and reporting.
- Building a successful cloud financial strategy requires a comprehensive approach that addresses cost management, financial governance, budgeting, forecasting, and performance monitoring.
- Organizations that embrace cloud financial best practices will be well-positioned to thrive in the competitive digital landscape, unlocking the full potential of cloud computing for growth and innovation.

3

BENEFITS AND CHALLENGES OF CLOUD-BASED FINANCIAL SYSTEMS

An image of a serene cloud-filled sky, with the clouds shaped like different financial tools and resources such as calculators, graphs, and spreadsheets.

I n today's fast-paced and ever-evolving business landscape, organizations constantly seek innovative solutions to streamline their operations, reduce costs, and enhance overall efficiency. One such groundbreaking development that has revolutionized the world of finance is the advent of cloud-based financial systems. As the name suggests, these systems leverage the power of cloud computing to provide a comprehensive, flexible, and scalable platform for managing an organization's financial operations. This chapter aims to provide a comprehensive understanding of cloud-based financial systems, their benefits, potential challenges, and strategies to overcome these challenges.

At its core, a cloud-based financial system is a software application that is **hosted on remote servers** and **accessed via the internet.** This means that instead of relying on traditional, on-premise software installations, organizations can now manage their financial operations from anywhere, at any time, and on any device with an internet connection. This paradigm shift has not only made financial management more accessible but has also opened up a plethora of opportunities for businesses to optimize their financial operations.

Cloud-based financial systems encompass a wide range of functionalities, including but not limited to accounting, budgeting, financial planning, reporting, and analysis. These systems can be customized to cater to the unique needs of different industries and organizations, making them an ideal solution for businesses of all sizes and types.

As we delve deeper into the world of cloud-based financial systems, it is essential to understand the various benefits and challenges associated with their implementation. In the following sections, we will explore the advantages of adopting cloud-based financial solutions, the potential risks and challenges that organizations may face, and the strategies that can be employed to overcome these challenges. Additionally, we will examine real-world examples of successful cloud financial implementations to provide a better understanding of the practical applications of these systems.

In conclusion, the future of financial management lies in

embracing the power of cloud-based financial systems. By understanding the benefits and challenges associated with these systems, organizations can make informed decisions and harness the potential of cloud technology to revolutionize their financial operations.

Advantages of Implementing Cloud-Based Financial Solutions

The rapid growth of cloud technology has revolutionized the way businesses manage their financial operations. Cloud-based financial solutions offer a myriad of advantages that can streamline processes, improve efficiency, and ultimately contribute to an organization's overall success. This section will delve into the key benefits of implementing cloud-based financial systems.

Cost Savings: One of the most significant advantages of cloud-based financial solutions is the potential for cost savings. Traditional on-premise systems often require substantial upfront investments in hardware, software, and infrastructure. In contrast, cloud-based solutions operate on a subscription-based model, eliminating the need for costly hardware and reducing the total cost of ownership. Additionally, cloud providers typically handle system maintenance and updates, further reducing the burden on internal IT resources.

Scalability: Cloud-based financial systems offer unparalleled scalability, allowing businesses to easily adjust their services according to their needs. As a company grows, it can quickly and seamlessly upgrade its cloud services to accommodate increased data storage and processing requirements. This flexibility ensures that organizations can adapt to changing market conditions and maintain a competitive edge.

Real-time Data Access: With cloud-based financial solutions, businesses can access their financial data in real time from any location with an internet connection. This enables faster decision-making and improved collaboration among team members, as they can work with up-to-date information regardless of their physical location. Real-time data access also allows for more accurate financial forecasting and reporting, leading to better-informed strategic decisions.

Enhanced Security: Contrary to popular belief, cloud-based financial systems can offer robust security measures that often surpass those of on-premise solutions. Cloud providers invest heavily in state-of-the-art security infrastructure and employ dedicated teams of experts to monitor and protect their systems. Additionally, cloud-based solutions typically include automatic data backup and disaster recovery capabilities, ensuring that critical financial information is safeguarded against potential threats.

Integration and Automation: Cloud-based financial systems can easily integrate with other cloud-based applications, such as customer relationship management (CRM) and enterprise resource planning (ERP) systems. This seamless integration facilitates the automation of various financial processes, such as invoicing, expense tracking, and payroll management. Automation not only saves time and reduces the risk of human error but also enables businesses to focus on more strategic tasks and initiatives.

Environmental Sustainability: By adopting cloud-based financial solutions, businesses can significantly reduce their carbon footprint. Cloud providers utilize energy-efficient data centers and often employ renewable energy sources, resulting in a more sustainable approach to managing financial operations. This benefits the environment, helps organizations meet their corporate social responsibility (CSR) goals, and enhances their reputation among customers and stakeholders.

In summary, implementing cloud-based financial solutions can provide businesses with numerous advantages, including cost savings, scalability, real-time data access, enhanced security, integration and automation, and environmental sustainability. By leveraging these benefits, organizations can streamline their financial operations, improve efficiency, and position themselves for long-term success in an increasingly competitive and technology-driven landscape.

Potential Risks and Challenges in Cloud Financial Operations

While cloud-based financial systems offer numerous benefits, it is essential to acknowledge and address the potential risks and challenges associated with their implementation. By understanding these concerns, organizations can make informed decisions and develop strategies to mitigate these risks. In this section, we will delve into the most common challenges faced by organizations when adopting cloud financial operations.

Data Security and Privacy: One of the most significant concerns for any organization considering cloud-based financial systems is the security and privacy of their sensitive financial data. Since cloud providers store data on remote servers, organizations must ensure that their chosen provider has robust security measures in place to protect against data breaches, unauthorized access, and other cyber threats. Additionally, organizations must comply with various data protection regulations, such as **GDPR** and **HIPAA**, which can be challenging to navigate in a cloud environment.

System Integration: Integrating a cloud-based financial system with existing on-premise systems and applications can be a complex and time-consuming process. Organizations must ensure seamless data flow and communication between the cloud and on-premise systems to avoid data silos and maintain operational efficiency. This may require significant investment in integration tools and expertise.

Downtime and Service Reliability: Cloud-based financial systems rely on the internet for access, which can lead to potential downtime and service disruptions due to network issues or provider outages. Organizations must evaluate the **service level agreements (SLAs)** of their cloud providers to ensure they meet their uptime and performance requirements. Additionally, having a contingency plan in place for service disruptions is crucial to minimize the impact on business operations.

Vendor Lock-In: When adopting a cloud-based financial system, organizations may become dependent on a single cloud provider for their financial operations. This can create challenges when attempting to switch providers or move back to an on-premise solution, as the process can be costly and time-consuming. Organizations should consider adopting a **multi-cloud strategy** to mitigate this risk or ensure their chosen provider offers flexible and open solutions that can easily integrate with other platforms.

Compliance and Regulatory Requirements: Financial organizations are subject to numerous compliance and regulatory requirements, which can be challenging to maintain in a cloud environment. Organizations must ensure their cloud provider adheres to industry-specific regulations and standards, such as **PCI DSS** for payment processing or **SOC 2** for financial reporting. Additionally, organizations must be prepared to demonstrate compliance with auditors and regulators, which may require additional documentation and reporting capabilities.

Cost Management: While cloud-based financial systems can offer cost savings through reduced infrastructure and maintenance expenses, organizations must carefully manage their cloud spending to avoid unexpected costs. This includes monitoring usage, optimizing resources, and selecting the most cost-effective cloud services and pricing models.

In conclusion, while cloud financial operations offer numerous benefits, organizations must be aware of the potential risks and challenges associated with their implementation. By understanding these concerns and developing strategies to address them, organizations can successfully adopt cloud-based financial systems and reap the rewards of increased efficiency, flexibility, and scalability.

Strategies for Overcoming Cloud-Based Financial System Challenges

As with any technological advancement, cloud-based financial systems come with their own set of challenges. However, these challenges can be effectively managed and overcome by adopting the right strategies. This section will explore various approaches to tackle the potential risks and difficulties associated with cloud financial operations.

Comprehensive Risk Assessment: Organizations should conduct a thorough risk assessment before implementing a cloud-based financial system. This process involves identifying potential threats, vulnerabilities, and the impact of these risks on the organization's financial operations. By understanding the risks, organizations can develop appropriate mitigation strategies and contingency plans to minimize the impact of these challenges.

Data Security and Privacy: Data security and privacy are critical concerns in cloud financial operations. To address these issues, organizations should implement robust security measures such as encryption, multi-factor authentication, and intrusion detection systems. Additionally, organizations should work closely with their cloud service providers to ensure they adhere to **strict security standards** and comply with relevant data protection regulations.

Regular System Audits: Conducting regular system audits can help organizations identify potential issues and vulnerabilities in their cloud-based financial systems. These audits should assess the effectiveness of security measures, data management practices, and overall system performance. By proactively identifying and addressing potential issues, organizations can minimize the risk of security breaches and system failures.

Employee Training and Awareness: One of the most significant challenges in cloud financial operations is the lack of employee awareness and understanding of the technology. To overcome this challenge, organizations should invest in comprehensive training programs to educate employees about the benefits, risks, and best practices associated with cloud-based financial systems. This will improve system adoption and help employees identify and report potential security threats.

Vendor Selection and Management: Choosing the right cloud service provider is crucial for the success of cloud financial operations. Organizations should carefully evaluate potential vendors based on their experience, security measures, and compliance with industry standards. Additionally, organizations should establish clear **service level agreements (SLAs)** with their vendors to ensure they meet performance expectations and provide timely support in case of issues.

Business Continuity Planning: To ensure the smooth functioning of cloud-based financial systems, organizations should develop comprehensive business continuity plans. These plans should outline the steps to be taken in case of system failures, data breaches, or other disruptions. By having a well-defined plan in place, organizations can minimize the impact of potential challenges and ensure the swift recovery of their financial operations.

In conclusion, while cloud-based financial systems offer numerous benefits, they also present certain challenges. By adopting the strategies outlined in this section, organizations can effectively manage these challenges and harness the full potential of cloud financial operations. As the world continues to embrace digital transformation, it is essential for businesses to stay ahead of the curve and adapt to the ever-evolving landscape of cloud-based financial systems.

Real-World Examples of Successful Cloud Financial Implementations

This section will explore real-world examples of organizations that have successfully implemented cloud-based financial systems. These examples will demonstrate the benefits and advantages that can be achieved by embracing cloud financial operations, as well as the strategies employed to overcome potential challenges.

Example 1: A Global Retail Company

A global retail company with thousands of stores across multiple countries faced challenges in managing its financial operations due to the disparate systems and processes in place. The company decided to implement a cloud-based financial system to streamline its operations, improve data accuracy, and reduce costs.

The implementation of the cloud-based financial system allowed the company to consolidate its financial data from various sources into a single platform. This enabled the company to generate real-time financial reports, improve budgeting and forecasting accuracy, and enhance decision-making capabilities. Additionally, the company was able to reduce its IT infrastructure costs and improve overall operational efficiency.

Example 2: A Non-Profit Organization

A non-profit organization with a limited budget and resources needed a cost-effective solution to manage its financial operations. The organization opted for a cloud-based financial system, which allowed it to access advanced financial tools and features without the need for significant upfront investments.

By implementing the cloud-based financial system, the non-profit organization was able to automate various financial processes, such as invoicing, expense tracking, and budgeting. This saved time and resources and improved the organization's financial transparency and accountability. The cloud-based system also provided the organization with real-time access to financial data, enabling it to make informed decisions and better allocate its limited resources.

Example 3: A Growing Tech Startup

A rapidly growing tech startup faced challenges in scaling its financial operations to keep up with its expanding business. So the startup decided to implement a cloud-based financial system to support its growth and enable seamless integration with other cloud-based business tools.

The cloud-based financial system provided the startup with a scalable and flexible solution that could easily adapt to its changing needs. The system allowed the company to automate various financial processes, such as payroll, invoicing, and expense management, which helped the startup save time and resources. Additionally, the cloud-based system offered advanced analytics and reporting capabilities, enabling the startup to gain valuable insights into its financial performance and make data-driven decisions.

In conclusion, these real-world examples demonstrate the potential benefits and advantages of implementing cloud-based financial systems. By leveraging cloud technology, organizations can streamline their financial operations, improve data accuracy, and reduce costs. Moreover, cloud-based financial systems offer scalability, flexibility, and advanced features that can help organizations adapt to changing business needs and drive growth. As we move towards the future, embracing cloud-based financial systems will become increasingly important for organizations looking to stay competitive and thrive in the digital age.

Embracing the Future of Cloud-Based Financial Systems

As we have explored throughout this chapter, cloud-based financial systems offer a myriad of benefits and opportunities for organizations of all sizes and industries. From increased efficiency and cost savings to enhanced security and scalability, the advantages of implementing cloud financial solutions are undeniable. However, as with any significant technological shift, there are also **potential risks** and challenges that must be addressed and mitigated.

Organizations must be proactive in their approach to cloud financial operations, ensuring that they clearly understand the potential risks and are prepared to address them. By developing comprehensive strategies for overcoming these challenges, businesses can confidently embrace the future of cloud-based financial systems and reap the rewards of this transformative technology.

As we have seen through real-world examples, successful cloud financial implementations can significantly improve an organization's overall financial performance. By leveraging the power of cloud technology, businesses can streamline their financial processes, gain valuable insights, and make data-driven decisions that drive growth and profitability.

In conclusion, the future of cloud-based financial systems is bright, and organizations that embrace this technology will be well-positioned to thrive in an increasingly competitive and complex global marketplace. By understanding the benefits and challenges of cloud financial operations and developing strategies to overcome these challenges, businesses can confidently move forward on their journey to a more efficient, secure, and scalable financial future.

As an author and industry expert, I encourage you to continue exploring the world of cloud-based financial systems and stay informed about the latest developments and best practices in this rapidly evolving field. By staying ahead of the curve, you can ensure your organization is prepared to capitalize on the many opportunities cloud financial technology offers.

Chapter Summary

- Cloud-based financial systems offer numerous benefits, including cost savings, scalability, real-time data access, enhanced security, integration and automation, and environmental sustainability.
- Potential risks and challenges associated with cloud financial operations include data security and privacy, system integration, downtime and service reliability, vendor lock-in, compliance and regulatory requirements, and cost management.
- Comprehensive risk assessment, robust data security measures, regular system audits, employee training and awareness, vendor selection and management, and business continuity planning are essential strategies for overcoming challenges in cloud-based financial systems.
- Real-world examples of successful cloud financial implementations demonstrate the potential benefits and advantages of adopting cloud-based financial systems, such as improved efficiency, data accuracy, and cost reduction.
- Cloud-based financial systems can be customized to cater to the unique needs of different industries and organizations, making them an ideal solution for businesses of all sizes and types.
- Seamless integration with other cloud-based applications, such as CRM and ERP systems, facilitates the automation of various financial processes, saving time and reducing the risk of human error.

- Organizations must be proactive in their approach to cloud financial operations, ensuring that they clearly understand the potential risks and are prepared to address them.
- Embracing cloud-based financial systems is crucial for organizations looking to stay competitive and thrive in the digital age, as they offer increased efficiency, security, and scalability for financial operations.

4

CLOUD FINANCIAL MANAGEMENT TOOLS AND PLATFORMS

A futuristic cityscape where buildings are connected by beams of light, symbolizing cloud computing networks.

In today's fast-paced and ever-evolving business landscape, organizations are increasingly turning to cloud-based solutions to streamline their financial operations and optimize their resources. As a result, cloud financial management tools and platforms have emerged as essential components of modern business strategies, offering a wide range of benefits and capabilities that traditional, on-premise systems cannot match.

At its core, cloud financial management refers to the process of managing an organization's financial resources, processes, and data using cloud-based tools and platforms. This approach allows businesses to access their financial information from anywhere at any time and to leverage the power of advanced analytics, automation, and real-time reporting to make more informed decisions and drive growth.

In this chapter, we will explore the world of cloud financial management tools and platforms, delving into their key features, comparing the top solutions available in the market, and providing insights on how to effectively integrate these tools into your business operations. We will also discuss best practices for implementing and optimizing cloud financial management, ensuring that you can maximize the benefits of these powerful solutions and propel your organization toward success.

As we embark on this journey, it is important to recognize that cloud financial management is not a one-size-fits-all solution. Each organization has its unique needs, goals, and challenges, and the right cloud financial management platform for one business may not be the best fit for another. Therefore, it is crucial to carefully evaluate the various options available and select the one that aligns with your specific requirements and objectives.

With that in mind, let's dive into the world of cloud financial management tools and platforms and discover how these innovative solutions can revolutionize your business operations and drive financial success.

Evaluating the Key Features of Cloud Financial Management Solutions

In today's fast-paced business environment, effective financial management is crucial for organizations of all sizes. As more companies migrate their financial operations to the cloud, it's essential to understand the key features of cloud financial management solutions and how they can benefit your organization. This section will explore the most important aspects to consider when evaluating these tools and platforms.

Scalability and Flexibility: One of the primary advantages of cloud-based financial management solutions is their ability to scale with your business. As your organization grows, your financial management needs will evolve, and a cloud-based solution should be able to accommodate this growth. Look for platforms that offer flexible pricing plans and the ability to add or remove features as needed.

Integration Capabilities: Your cloud financial management solution should seamlessly integrate with your existing systems and applications, such as your ERP, CRM, and other financial tools. This will ensure a smooth data flow between systems, reducing manual data entry and the risk of errors. Additionally, integration with third-party applications can help streamline your financial processes and provide a more comprehensive view of your organization's financial health.

Security and Compliance: Protecting your financial data is paramount, and cloud financial management solutions should offer robust security measures to keep your information safe. Look for platforms with strong encryption, multi-factor authentication, and regular security audits. Additionally, ensure the solution complies with relevant industry regulations, such as **GDPR, HIPAA,** or **SOC 2.**

Real-Time Reporting and Analytics: Access to real-time financial data is essential for making informed business decisions. Your cloud financial management solution should provide customizable dashboards and reports that allow you to monitor key performance indicators (KPIs) and gain insights into your organization's financial health. Advanced analytics capabilities can help you identify trends, uncover inefficiencies, and make data-driven decisions to improve your financial operations.

Automation and Workflow Management: Streamlining your financial processes can save time, reduce errors, and improve overall efficiency. Look for cloud financial management solutions that offer automation features, such as automated invoicing, expense tracking, and reconciliation. Workflow management tools can also help you establish approval processes, assign tasks, and monitor progress, ensuring your financial operations run smoothly and efficiently.

User Experience and Accessibility: A user-friendly interface ensures your team can effectively utilize the cloud financial management solution. Look for platforms with intuitive navigation, clear instructions, and easily accessible support resources. Additionally, consider solutions that offer mobile access, allowing your team to manage financial tasks and access data from anywhere at any time.

Customer Support and Training: Implementing a new financial management solution can be a complex process, and having access to reliable customer support is crucial. Choose a platform with a strong reputation for providing timely, knowledgeable assistance. Additionally, consider the availability of training resources, such as webinars, tutorials, and documentation, to help your team get up to speed quickly.

In conclusion, evaluating the key features of cloud financial management solutions is a critical step in choosing the right platform for your organization. By considering factors such as scalability, integration capabilities, security, reporting, automation, user experience, and support, you can select a solution that will streamline your financial operations and drive growth for your business.

Comparing Top Cloud Financial Management Platforms

In today's rapidly evolving digital landscape, choosing the right cloud financial management platform is crucial for businesses to stay competitive and maintain **financial agility**. With a plethora of options available in the market, it can be overwhelming to determine which platform best suits your organization's needs. This section will compare some of the top cloud financial management platforms, highlighting their key features, strengths, and weaknesses to help you make an informed decision.

Oracle NetSuite: As a comprehensive cloud financial management solution, Oracle NetSuite offers a wide range of features, including financial planning, reporting, and analytics. Its robust capabilities cater to businesses of all sizes and industries. NetSuite's strengths lie in its **scalability, user-friendly interface, and seamless integration** with other Oracle products. However, the platform's pricing may be on the higher side for smaller businesses, and some users have reported occasional performance issues.

Sage Intacct: Sage Intacct is a popular choice for small to medium-sized businesses, offering a powerful suite of financial management tools. Its core features include accounts payable, accounts receivable, cash management, and financial reporting. Sage Intacct stands out for its **flexible and customizable reporting capabilities,** as well as its user-friendly interface. On the downside, the platform may lack some advanced features required by larger enterprises, and its integration with third-party applications can be limited.

Workday Adaptive Planning: Workday Adaptive Planning is a cloud-based financial planning and analysis platform that caters to businesses of all sizes. Its key features include budgeting, forecasting, reporting, and analytics. The platform is known for its **intuitive user interface, powerful modeling capabilities, and seamless integration** with other Workday products. However, some users have reported challenges with the platform's learning curve and occasional performance issues.

Microsoft Dynamics 365 Finance: Microsoft Dynamics 365 Finance is a comprehensive cloud financial management solution that integrates seamlessly with other Microsoft products. Its core features include general ledger, accounts payable, accounts receivable, and financial reporting. The platform's strengths include its **robust functionality, scalability, and strong integration capabilities.** However, some users have reported a steep learning curve and challenges with customization.

QuickBooks Online: QuickBooks Online is a popular choice for small businesses, offering a user-friendly cloud financial management solution. Its key features include invoicing, expense tracking, and financial reporting. The platform is known for its ease of use, **affordability, and integration** with various third-party applications. However, QuickBooks Online may not be suitable for larger enterprises or those requiring advanced financial management features.

When comparing these top cloud financial management platforms, it is essential to consider factors such as your organization's size, industry, and specific financial management requirements. Additionally, consider the platform's **ease of use, integration capabilities**, and **scalability** to ensure that it can grow with your business. By carefully evaluating each platform's strengths and weaknesses, you can select the most suitable solution to optimize your cloud financial operations and drive business success.

Integrating Cloud Financial Management Tools into Your Business Operations

In today's fast-paced business environment, organizations need to have a robust and efficient financial management system in place. Cloud financial management tools and platforms offer a comprehensive solution to streamline financial operations, reduce costs, and improve decision-making. This section will discuss the steps involved in integrating cloud financial management tools into your business operations and how to ensure a smooth transition.

Assess your current financial management system: Before you can integrate a cloud financial management tool into your business operations, it is crucial to evaluate your existing financial management system. Identify the strengths and weaknesses of your current system, and determine the specific areas where a cloud-based solution can add value. This will help you choose the right tool for your organization's unique needs and requirements.

Choose the right cloud financial management platform: With numerous cloud financial management tools and platforms available in the market, it is essential to select the one that best aligns with your business objectives and requirements. When comparing different platforms, consider factors such as ease of use, scalability, integration capabilities, and security features. Additionally, look for a solution that offers robust reporting and analytics features to help you make data-driven decisions.

Develop a detailed implementation plan: Once you have chosen the right cloud financial management platform, develop a comprehensive implementation plan that outlines the steps and timelines for integrating the tool into your business operations. This plan should include tasks such as data migration, system configuration, user training, and testing. Make sure to involve all relevant stakeholders in the planning process to ensure a smooth transition.

Train your team: In order to maximize the benefits of your new cloud financial management tool, it is essential to train your team on how to use the platform effectively. Provide comprehensive training sessions that cover the key features and functionalities of the tool, as well as any specific processes and workflows relevant to your organization. Encourage your team to ask questions and provide feedback to ensure they are comfortable using the new system.

Monitor and optimize: After implementing the cloud financial management platform, continuously monitor its performance and effectiveness. Gather feedback from your team and analyze key performance indicators (KPIs) to identify areas for improvement. Regularly update and optimize the system to ensure it continues to meet your organization's evolving needs and requirements.

Leverage the power of integration: One of the significant advantages of cloud financial management tools is their ability to integrate with other business applications and systems. Explore the integration capabilities of your chosen platform and connect it with your existing tools, such as CRM, ERP, and HR systems. This will help you streamline your financial operations and improve overall efficiency.

By following these steps, you can successfully integrate a cloud financial management tool into your business operations and unlock its full potential. Embrace the power of cloud technology to transform your financial management processes, drive cost savings, and make informed decisions that propel your organization toward success.

Best Practices for Implementing and Optimizing Cloud Financial Management

As businesses continue to embrace cloud technology, it is crucial to adopt best practices for implementing and optimizing cloud financial management. By following these guidelines, organizations can maximize the benefits of cloud financial management tools and platforms, ensuring a seamless and efficient transition to the cloud. This section will discuss several best practices that can help businesses succeed in their cloud financial management journey.

Develop a comprehensive cloud financial management strategy: Before implementing any cloud financial management tools or platforms, it is essential to develop a well-defined strategy that aligns with your organization's overall business objectives. This strategy should include a clear understanding of your current financial processes, the desired outcomes from adopting cloud financial management, and the key performance indicators (KPIs) that will be used to measure success.

Choose the right cloud financial management platform: With numerous cloud financial management solutions available in the market, selecting the right platform for your organization can be challenging. To make an informed decision, evaluate each platform based on its features, scalability, ease of integration, and cost. Additionally, consider the platform's ability to support your organization's unique requirements and industry-specific regulations.

Establish a cross-functional implementation team: Implementing a cloud financial management platform requires collaboration between various departments within your organization, such as finance, IT, and operations. Establish a cross-functional team that includes representatives from each of these departments to ensure a smooth implementation process and to address any potential challenges that may arise.

Invest in employee training and change management: The success of your cloud financial management implementation largely depends on the adoption and proficiency of your employees. Therefore, invest in comprehensive training programs to help your team understand the new tools and processes. Additionally, develop a change management plan to address any resistance to change and to ensure a smooth transition to the new system.

Regularly monitor and optimize your cloud financial management processes: Once your cloud financial management platform is up and running, it is essential to continuously monitor its performance and optimize processes to ensure maximum efficiency. Regularly review your KPIs, identify areas for improvement, and make necessary adjustments to your cloud financial management strategy.

Leverage automation and artificial intelligence (AI): Many cloud financial management platforms offer automation and AI capabilities that can significantly improve efficiency and reduce manual tasks. Identify processes within your organization that can benefit from automation and AI, and leverage these features to streamline your financial operations.

Ensure data security and compliance: Data security and regulatory compliance are critical aspects of cloud financial management. Work closely with your IT department and platform provider to implement robust security measures and ensure that your organization remains compliant with industry-specific regulations.

Foster a culture of continuous improvement: Cloud financial management is an ongoing process that requires constant evaluation and improvement. Encourage continuous improvement within your organization by regularly reviewing your cloud financial management strategy, soliciting employee feedback, and staying informed about industry trends and best practices.

In conclusion, implementing and optimizing cloud financial management tools and platforms can significantly improve your organization's financial operations and overall efficiency. By following these best practices, you can ensure a successful transition to the cloud and maximize the benefits of cloud financial management for your business.

Maximizing the Benefits of Cloud Financial Management Tools and Platforms

In today's fast-paced and ever-evolving business landscape, cloud financial management tools and platforms have emerged as indispensable assets for organizations seeking to optimize their financial operations. By leveraging the power of these innovative solutions, businesses can streamline their financial processes, gain valuable insights, and make data-driven decisions that drive growth and profitability.

In order to maximize the benefits of cloud financial management tools and platforms, it is essential to adopt a strategic and holistic approach. This entails selecting the right solution for your organization and ensuring seamless integration, effective implementation, and continuous optimization.

First and foremost, it is crucial to thoroughly evaluate the available cloud financial management solutions in the market. This involves assessing their key features, such as automation capabilities, real-time reporting, and scalability, to determine which platform best aligns with your organization's needs and objectives. Additionally, it is important to consider factors such as cost, ease of use, and vendor support when making your decision.

Once you have selected the ideal cloud financial management platform for your business, the next step is to integrate it into your existing operations. This may involve migrating data from legacy systems, configuring the platform to align with your organization's unique processes, and training your team to utilize the new tools effectively. By ensuring a smooth transition, you can minimize disruptions and set the stage for long-term success.

Implementation is only the beginning of your cloud financial management journey. To truly reap the benefits of these powerful tools and platforms, it is essential to continuously optimize your financial operations. This may involve refining your processes, leveraging advanced analytics to uncover new insights, and staying up-to-date on industry best practices. Adopting a **proactive and iterative approach** ensures that your organization remains at the forefront of financial management innovation.

In conclusion, cloud financial management tools and platforms offer a wealth of opportunities for organizations looking to enhance their financial operations. By carefully evaluating, integrating, implementing, and optimizing these solutions, businesses can unlock their full potential and achieve new levels of efficiency, agility, and growth. As an author and industry expert, I encourage you to embrace the power of cloud financial management and embark on a journey toward a more prosperous and sustainable future.

Chapter Summary

- Cloud financial management tools and platforms are essential to modern business strategies, offering benefits such as advanced analytics, automation, and real-time reporting.
- Key features to consider when evaluating cloud financial management solutions include scalability, integration capabilities, security, real-time reporting, automation, user experience, and customer support.
- Comparing top cloud financial management platforms, such as Oracle NetSuite, Sage Intacct, Workday Adaptive Planning, Microsoft Dynamics 365 Finance, and QuickBooks Online, can help businesses choose the right solution for their needs.
- Integrating cloud financial management tools into business operations involves assessing the current financial management system, choosing the right platform, developing an implementation plan, training the team, monitoring and optimizing the system, and leveraging integration capabilities.

- Best practices for implementing and optimizing cloud financial management include developing a comprehensive strategy, choosing the right platform, establishing a cross-functional implementation team, investing in employee training and change management, regularly monitoring and optimizing processes, leveraging automation and AI, ensuring data security and compliance, and fostering a culture of continuous improvement.
- Adopting a strategic and holistic approach to cloud financial management can help businesses maximize the benefits of these innovative solutions.
- Continuous optimization of financial operations is crucial for reaping the full benefits of cloud financial management tools and platforms.
- Embracing the power of cloud financial management can help organizations enhance their financial operations, achieve new levels of efficiency, agility, and growth, and ultimately drive success.

5

SECURITY AND COMPLIANCE IN CLOUD FINANCIAL OPERATIONS

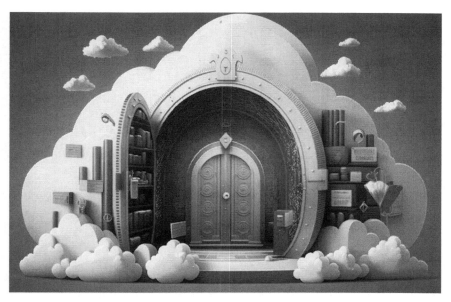

An image of a cloud in the form of a giant vault, with its door opening to reveal a treasure trove of financial assets.

In today's digital age, businesses are increasingly relying on cloud-based solutions to streamline their financial operations. The adoption of cloud financial operations offers numerous benefits, including cost reduction, increased efficiency, and improved accessibility. However, with these advantages comes the critical responsibility of ensuring the security and compliance of sensitive financial data. This chapter will explore the importance of security and compliance in cloud financial operations, discuss key regulations and standards, and provide guidance on implementing robust security measures and best practices.

As organizations transition their financial operations to the cloud, they must navigate a complex landscape of security risks and compliance requirements. The stakes are high, as financial data is often a prime target for cybercriminals due to its sensitive nature and potential for financial gain. Additionally, organizations must adhere to a myriad of industry-specific regulations and standards to avoid costly fines and reputational damage.

In this context, security and compliance are not merely checkboxes to be ticked off but essential components of a successful cloud financial operations strategy. By understanding the risks and requirements associated with cloud financial operations, organizations can implement effective security measures and controls to protect their data and maintain compliance with relevant regulations and standards.

In the following sections, we will delve deeper into the importance of data security in cloud financial operations, explore key compliance regulations and standards, discuss the implementation of robust security measures and controls, and provide best practices for ensuring a secure and compliant cloud financial operations environment. By the end of this chapter, you will have a solid understanding of the critical role that security and compliance play in the success of your cloud financial operations and be equipped with the knowledge and tools necessary to safeguard your organization's financial data.

Understanding the Importance of Data Security in Cloud Financial Operations

In today's digital age, data has become the lifeblood of modern businesses. As organizations increasingly rely on cloud-based solutions to manage their financial operations, ensuring the security and integrity of their data has never been more critical. This section will delve into the importance of data security in cloud financial operations and why it should be a top priority for businesses of all sizes.

First and foremost, **data security** is essential for maintaining the trust and confidence of customers, partners, and stakeholders. As financial data often includes sensitive information such as bank account details, credit card numbers, and personal identification information, any breach or unauthorized access can have severe consequences. A single security incident can tarnish a company's reputation, leading to a loss of customers, revenue, and even legal repercussions.

Moreover, data breaches can result in significant financial losses for businesses. According to a study by IBM, the average cost of a data breach in 2020 was $3.86 million, with the financial industry experiencing even higher costs. These losses can stem from various factors, including fines and penalties, legal fees, customer compensation, and the expenses of investigating and remediating the breach.

Compliance with industry regulations and standards is another crucial aspect of data security in cloud financial operations. Organizations must adhere to various laws and guidelines, such as the **General Data Protection Regulation (GDPR)**, the **Payment Card Industry Data Security Standard (PCI DSS)**, and the **Sarbanes-Oxley Act (SOX)**. Non-compliance can result in hefty fines, legal actions, and damage to a company's reputation.

Furthermore, robust data security measures can provide businesses with a competitive advantage. As customers become more aware of the risks associated with data breaches, they are more likely to choose providers that prioritize security and demonstrate a strong commitment to protecting their information. By investing in advanced security measures and adhering to industry best practices, organizations can differentiate themselves from competitors and build long-lasting **customer relationships.**

Lastly, data security is essential for ensuring the smooth functioning of cloud financial operations. A secure environment enables businesses to operate efficiently and make informed decisions based on accurate and reliable data. In contrast, a compromised system can lead to inaccurate financial reporting, disrupted operations, and poor decision-making.

In conclusion, understanding the importance of data security in cloud financial operations is crucial for businesses to protect their sensitive information, maintain trust with customers and partners, comply with industry regulations, and ensure the smooth functioning of their operations. By prioritizing data security, organizations can safeguard their financial data and build a strong foundation for success in the digital age.

Key Compliance Regulations and Standards for Cloud Financial Operations

In today's digital age, ensuring the security and compliance of financial data is of paramount importance. As organizations increasingly adopt cloud-based financial operations, they must adhere to various regulatory requirements and industry standards to protect sensitive financial information and maintain the trust of their clients and stakeholders. This section will discuss the key compliance regulations and standards that organizations must consider when implementing cloud financial operations.

General Data Protection Regulation (GDPR): The **GDPR** is a comprehensive data protection regulation that affects organizations operating within the European Union (EU) or processing the personal data of EU citizens. It aims to strengthen personal data protection and give individuals greater control over their information. Organizations handling financial data in the cloud must ensure that their operations are GDPR-compliant, which includes implementing appropriate security measures, obtaining user consent, and reporting data breaches within 72 hours.

Payment Card Industry Data Security Standard (PCI DSS): The **PCI DSS** is a set of security standards designed to ensure that all organizations that accept, process, store, or transmit credit card information maintain a secure environment. Cloud financial operations that involve cardholder data must adhere to these standards, which include requirements for network security, data encryption, access control, and vulnerability management.

Sarbanes-Oxley Act (SOX): The Sarbanes-Oxley Act is a US federal law that aims to protect investors by improving the accuracy and reliability of corporate financial disclosures. Organizations that are subject to **SOX** must ensure that their cloud financial operations maintain proper internal controls and procedures for financial reporting. This includes implementing access controls, data integrity measures, and audit trails to ensure the accuracy and security of financial data.

Health Insurance Portability and Accountability Act (HIPAA): Although primarily focused on the healthcare industry, **HIPAA** also has implications for cloud financial operations that handle protected health information (PHI) in the context of billing and payment processing. Organizations subject to HIPAA must ensure that their cloud financial operations maintain PHI's confidentiality, integrity, and availability by implementing appropriate administrative, physical, and technical safeguards.

International Organization for Standardization (ISO) Standards: The **ISO** has developed several standards that are relevant to cloud financial operations, including ISO/IEC 27001 for information security management systems and ISO/IEC 27017 for cloud security. These standards provide a framework for implementing, maintaining, and improving the security of cloud financial operations, and achieving certification can help organizations demonstrate their commitment to security and compliance.

Financial Industry Regulatory Authority (FINRA): FINRA is a non-governmental organization that regulates brokerage firms and their registered representatives in the United States. It has issued guidelines for the use of cloud services in the financial industry, which emphasize the importance of due diligence, risk assessment, and ongoing monitoring of cloud service providers. Organizations subject to FINRA regulations must ensure that their cloud financial operations adhere to these guidelines and maintain appropriate security and compliance measures.

In conclusion, organizations implementing cloud financial operations must navigate a complex landscape of regulatory requirements and industry standards. By understanding and adhering to these key compliance regulations and standards, organizations can ensure the security and integrity of their financial data, maintain the trust of their clients, and avoid costly penalties and reputational damage.

Implementing Robust Security Measures and Controls in Cloud Financial Operations

In today's digital age, ensuring the security and privacy of financial data is of paramount importance. With the increasing adoption of cloud-based financial operations, businesses must implement robust security measures and controls to protect sensitive information and maintain compliance with industry regulations. This section will delve into the various security measures and controls that organizations can implement to safeguard their cloud financial operations.

Data Encryption: Encrypting data at rest and in transit is a crucial security measure for cloud financial operations. By using strong encryption algorithms, businesses can ensure that their financial data remains unreadable even if it falls into the wrong hands. It is essential to choose a cloud service provider that offers robust encryption options and key management capabilities.

Identity and Access Management (IAM): Implementing a comprehensive IAM system helps organizations control who has access to their cloud financial operations. This includes setting up multi-factor authentication (MFA), defining user roles and permissions, and regularly reviewing access logs to detect any unauthorized activity. IAM systems should also be integrated with the organization's existing security infrastructure to ensure seamless and secure access to cloud financial services.

Network Security: Securing the network infrastructure is vital for protecting cloud financial operations from external threats. This involves deploying firewalls, intrusion detection and prevention systems (IDPS), and virtual private networks (VPNs) to safeguard the network perimeter. Additionally, organizations should regularly conduct vulnerability assessments and penetration testing to identify and remediate potential security gaps.

Security Monitoring and Incident Response: Continuous monitoring of cloud financial operations is essential for detecting and responding to security incidents in real-time. By implementing a security information and event management (SIEM) system, organizations can collect, analyze, and correlate security events from various sources, enabling them to identify potential threats and take appropriate action. A well-defined incident response plan should also be in place to guide the organization's response to security incidents and minimize their impact on business operations.

Data Backup and Disaster Recovery: Regularly backing up financial data and having a disaster recovery plan in place is crucial for ensuring business continuity in the event of a security breach or system failure. Organizations should choose a cloud service provider that offers reliable backup and recovery options and test their disaster recovery plan periodically to ensure its effectiveness.

Security Awareness and Training: Educating employees about the importance of security and their role in protecting the organization's financial data is essential for maintaining a secure cloud financial operations environment. Regular security awareness training should be provided to all employees, and specific training should be given to those directly involved in managing and accessing cloud financial services.

By implementing these robust security measures and controls, organizations can significantly reduce the risk of security breaches and maintain compliance with industry regulations. Ultimately, a secure and compliant cloud financial operations environment will enable businesses to reap the benefits of cloud technology while safeguarding their sensitive financial data.

Best Practices for Ensuring Security and Compliance in Cloud Financial Operations

In today's digital age, ensuring the security and compliance of your cloud financial operations is paramount. With the increasing number of cyber threats and the ever-evolving landscape of regulatory requirements, organizations must adopt a proactive approach to safeguard their sensitive financial data and maintain compliance. This section will discuss some best practices that can help you achieve a secure and compliant cloud financial operations environment.

Develop a comprehensive security and compliance strategy: Before implementing any security measures, it is crucial to have a well-defined strategy in place. This should include a thorough risk assessment, identifying key compliance requirements, and clearly understanding your organization's security objectives. A comprehensive strategy will serve as a roadmap for implementing effective security controls and ensuring ongoing compliance.

Choose a reputable cloud service provider: The security and compliance of your cloud financial operations largely depend on the capabilities of your chosen cloud service provider. Ensure that the provider has a **strong track record** in security and compliance, and offers robust security features such as encryption, access controls, and intrusion detection systems. Additionally, verify that the provider is compliant with relevant industry standards and regulations.

Implement strong access controls: Restricting access to sensitive financial data is critical to maintaining security and compliance. Implement role-based access controls to ensure only authorized personnel can access specific data and resources. Additionally, enforce strong authentication mechanisms, such as multi-factor authentication, to prevent unauthorized access.

Encrypt sensitive data: Encryption is a powerful tool for protecting sensitive financial data at rest and in transit. Ensure that your cloud service provider offers robust encryption options, and use encryption keys that are managed and stored securely.

Regularly monitor and audit your cloud environment: Continuous monitoring and auditing of your cloud financial operations are essential for identifying potential security threats and ensuring compliance with regulatory requirements. Implement monitoring tools to track user activities, access logs, and system configurations. Additionally, conduct regular audits to assess the effectiveness of your security controls and identify areas for improvement.

Establish a robust incident response plan: Security breaches can still occur despite your best efforts. Having a well-defined incident response plan in place will help you quickly identify, contain, and remediate security incidents, minimizing their impact on your organization. Ensure that your plan includes clear roles and responsibilities, communication protocols, and a process for reporting and documenting incidents.

Stay informed about regulatory changes and emerging threats: The landscape of security threats and compliance requirements is constantly evolving. Stay informed about the latest developments in your industry and update your security and compliance strategy accordingly. Regularly review and update your security policies and procedures to ensure they effectively address new risks and compliance obligations.

Train and educate your employees: Your employees play a critical role in maintaining the security and compliance of your cloud financial operations. Provide regular training and education to ensure they know their responsibilities and the latest security best practices. Encourage a culture of security awareness and accountability within your organization.

In conclusion, achieving a secure and compliant cloud financial operations environment requires a proactive and ongoing effort. By following these best practices and working closely with your cloud service provider, you can effectively safeguard your sensitive financial data and maintain compliance with relevant industry standards and regulations.

Achieving a Secure and Compliant Cloud Financial Operations Environment

In conclusion, security and compliance are critical aspects of cloud financial operations that organizations must prioritize to protect their sensitive financial data and adhere to the various regulatory requirements. As the world becomes increasingly interconnected and reliant on cloud-based solutions, the need for robust security measures and compliance strategies will only continue to grow.

Achieving a secure and compliant cloud financial operations environment requires a comprehensive approach that encompasses understanding the importance of data security, staying informed about key compliance regulations and standards, implementing robust security measures and controls, and following best practices.

Organizations must invest in continuous **employee education and training** to ensure they are well-versed in the latest security and compliance requirements. Additionally, fostering a culture of security awareness and compliance within the organization can help create a proactive approach to identifying and addressing potential risks.

Collaboration between various departments, including IT, finance, and legal, is essential for developing a cohesive security and compliance strategy. By working together, these teams can identify potential vulnerabilities, assess risks, and implement appropriate controls to safeguard the organization's financial data.

Leveraging **advanced technologies**, such as artificial intelligence and machine learning, can also help organizations stay ahead of emerging threats and enhance their security posture. Furthermore, partnering with reputable cloud service providers that prioritize security and compliance can provide additional layers of protection and support.

Regular audits and assessments are crucial for ensuring that security measures and compliance policies remain effective and up-to-date. Organizations should also be prepared to adapt and evolve their strategies as new regulations emerge and the threat landscape changes.

In summary, achieving a secure and compliant cloud financial operations environment is an ongoing process that demands constant vigilance, collaboration, and adaptation. By prioritizing security and compliance, organizations can protect their valuable financial data and maintain the trust and confidence of their customers, partners, and regulators. As an author and industry expert, I encourage organizations to embrace the challenges and opportunities presented by cloud financial operations and strive for continuous improvement in their security and compliance efforts.

Chapter Summary

- Security and compliance are critical components of a successful cloud financial operations strategy, as they protect sensitive financial data and ensure adherence to industry regulations and standards.
- Data security in cloud financial operations is essential for maintaining trust with customers and partners, ensuring the smooth functioning of operations, and complying with industry regulations.
- Key compliance regulations and standards for cloud financial operations include GDPR, PCI DSS, SOX, HIPAA, ISO standards, and FINRA guidelines.
- Implementing robust security measures and controls, such as data encryption, identity and access management, network security, security monitoring, and incident response, is crucial for safeguarding cloud financial operations.
- Best practices for ensuring security and compliance in cloud financial operations include developing a comprehensive strategy, choosing a reputable cloud service provider, implementing strong access controls, encrypting sensitive data, and regularly monitoring and auditing the cloud environment.

- Establishing a robust incident response plan and staying informed about regulatory changes and emerging threats are essential for maintaining a secure and compliant cloud financial operations environment.
- Training and educating employees on security and compliance responsibilities and fostering a culture of security awareness are crucial for maintaining a secure cloud financial operations environment.
- Achieving a secure and compliant cloud financial operations environment requires ongoing vigilance, collaboration, and adaptation, as well as leveraging advanced technologies and partnering with reputable cloud service providers

6

**COST OPTIMIZATION STRATEGIES
FOR CLOUD FINANCE**

An image illustrating the seamless integration of cloud-based financial systems with various devices.

I n today's fast-paced and ever-evolving digital landscape, businesses increasingly adopt cloud-based solutions to stream-line their operations, enhance scalability, and improve overall efficiency. As organizations migrate their financial operations to the cloud, it becomes imperative to optimize costs and ensure that resources are utilized effectively. This chapter delves into the world of cost optimization strategies for cloud finance, providing valuable insights and practical tips for businesses looking to maximize the return on their cloud investments.

Cost optimization in cloud finance refers to the process of **minimizing expenses** associated with cloud-based financial operations while maintaining or improving performance, reliability, and security. It involves a comprehensive understanding of the organization's cloud usage patterns, identifying inefficiencies, and implementing strategic measures to reduce costs without compromising quality or functionality. The ultimate goal is to strike a balance between cost savings and operational efficiency, ensuring that the organization's financial operations are agile, scalable, and cost-effective.

As cloud adoption continues to grow, businesses must proactively manage their cloud expenditure. This requires a holistic approach, encompassing not only the technical aspects of cloud infrastructure but also the financial management and planning aspects. By implementing cost optimization strategies, organizations can achieve significant savings, freeing up resources to invest in innovation and growth.

In this chapter, we will explore various cost optimization strategies for cloud finance, including assessing and analyzing cloud expenditure, right-sizing and resource allocation, leveraging reserved instances and savings plans, and utilizing automation and monitoring tools. By following these best practices, businesses can ensure that their cloud financial operations are efficient, cost-effective, and aligned with their strategic objectives.

As we navigate the world of cost optimization in cloud finance, we must remember that every organization's needs and requirements are unique. Therefore, it is crucial to tailor these strategies to your specific business context, considering factors such as industry, size, and growth trajectory. With a clear understanding of your organization's cloud financial landscape and a commitment to continuous improvement, you can unlock the full potential of cloud finance and drive your business forward.

Assessing and Analyzing Cloud Expenditure

In today's fast-paced digital world, businesses are increasingly turning to cloud-based solutions to streamline their operations and reduce costs. However, without a clear understanding of cloud expenditure, organizations may struggle to optimize their financial performance. This section will discuss the importance of assessing and analyzing cloud expenditure and provide practical tips to help you gain better control over your cloud finances.

First, it is essential to recognize that cloud expenditure is not a one-time cost. Instead, it is an ongoing expense that requires continuous monitoring and management. This is because cloud service providers typically offer a pay-as-you-go pricing model, meaning your costs will vary depending on your usage patterns and the specific services you choose to utilize.

To effectively assess and analyze your cloud expenditure, you should start by gathering detailed information about your current usage and costs. This can be achieved through manual data collection and automated reporting tools provided by your cloud service provider. Some key metrics to track include the following:

- **Total cloud spend:** This is the overall amount you spend on cloud services, including infrastructure, storage, and data transfer costs.
- **Cost per service:** Break down your total cloud spend by individual service, such as compute instances, storage, and databases, to identify areas where you may be overspending or underutilizing resources.

- **Usage patterns:** Analyze your usage data to identify trends and patterns that may be driving up your costs. For example, you may find that certain services are only used during specific times of the day or week, which could present opportunities for cost optimization.
- **Cost per user or department:** If your organization has multiple users or departments accessing cloud services, tracking costs on a per-user or per-department basis can be helpful. This will enable you to pinpoint areas where spending may be excessive and identify opportunities for cost-sharing or chargeback models.

Once you clearly understand your current cloud expenditure, you can identify areas for improvement and implement cost optimization strategies. This may involve right-sizing your resources, leveraging reserved instances and savings plans, or utilizing automation and monitoring tools to ensure that you only **pay for the services you need**.

In conclusion, assessing and analyzing your cloud expenditure is a critical first step in optimizing your cloud financial operations. By gaining a comprehensive understanding of your current spending patterns and identifying areas for improvement, you can make informed decisions that will ultimately lead to greater financial efficiency in the cloud.

Implementing Right-Sizing and Resource Allocation

One of the most effective ways to optimize costs in cloud finance is by implementing right-sizing and resource allocation strategies. In this section, we will explore the importance of these strategies, the steps involved in right-sizing your cloud resources, and how to allocate resources efficiently to achieve maximum cost savings.

Right-sizing is the process of matching the capacity and performance of cloud resources to the actual needs of your applications and workloads. This ensures that you are not over-provisioning resources, which can lead to unnecessary costs or under-provisioning resources, which can result in performance issues and unhappy customers. By right-sizing your cloud resources, you can balance cost and performance, ensuring that you only pay for what you need.

To implement right-sizing in your cloud environment, follow these steps:

- **Assess your current resource usage:** Begin by analyzing your current cloud resource usage, including CPU, memory, storage, and network bandwidth. This will help you identify areas where resources are over or under-utilized.
- **Identify opportunities for optimization:** Once you clearly understand your current resource usage, look for opportunities to optimize. This may include consolidating instances, resizing instances to better match workload requirements, or moving workloads to more cost-effective services.
- **Implement changes and monitor results:** After identifying optimization opportunities, implement the necessary changes and monitor the results. This will help you validate that the changes have had the desired effect on cost and performance and allow you to make any necessary adjustments.

Resource allocation is another critical aspect of cost optimization in cloud finance. Efficient resource allocation ensures that you are making the most of your cloud investment by distributing resources in a way that maximizes performance and minimizes costs. To achieve this, consider the following strategies:

- **Use auto-scaling:** Auto-scaling allows you to automatically adjust the number of instances or resources based on demand. This ensures that you always have the right amount of resources to meet your needs without over-provisioning or under-provisioning.

- **Implement load balancing:** Load balancing distributes traffic across multiple instances, ensuring that no single instance becomes a bottleneck. This not only improves performance but also allows you to make better use of your resources, reducing costs.
- **Leverage multi-cloud and hybrid cloud strategies:** By utilizing multiple cloud providers or a combination of on-premises and cloud resources, you can take advantage of the best pricing and performance options available, further optimizing your resource allocation and cost.
- **Optimize storage and data management:** Efficiently managing your data storage and transfer can significantly impact your cloud costs. Consider using data compression, deduplication, and caching to reduce storage and data transfer costs.
- **Continuously review and adjust:** Regularly review your resource allocation and make adjustments as needed to ensure that you always make the most of your cloud investment.

In conclusion, right-sizing and resource allocation are essential strategies for cost optimization in cloud finance. By carefully assessing your resource usage, identifying optimization opportunities, and efficiently allocating resources, you can achieve significant cost savings while maintaining the performance and reliability your customers expect.

Leveraging Reserved Instances and Savings Plans

In today's competitive business landscape, organizations constantly seek ways to reduce costs and optimize their cloud financial operations. One of the most effective strategies for achieving this is by leveraging **Reserved Instances (RIs)** and Savings Plans. This section will explore how these two cost-saving mechanisms can help organizations achieve financial efficiency in the cloud.

Reserved Instances (RIs) are a pricing model offered by cloud service providers that allow organizations to reserve compute capacity for a specific period, typically one or three years. By committing to longer-term usage, organizations can enjoy significant discounts on their cloud infrastructure costs compared to on-demand pricing. RIs can be an excellent option for organizations with predictable workloads and long-term cloud usage requirements.

To maximize the benefits of RIs, organizations should carefully analyze their historical usage patterns and forecast future needs. This will enable them to make informed decisions about the appropriate instance types, sizes, and durations to reserve. Additionally, organizations should regularly review their RI utilization to ensure they fully leverage their reserved capacity and make necessary adjustments as their needs evolve.

Savings Plans, on the other hand, are a more flexible cost optimization mechanism that allows organizations to commit to a specific level of compute usage, measured in dollars per hour, for a one or three-year term. In exchange for this commitment, organizations receive discounts on their cloud infrastructure costs. Savings Plans can be applied to a wide range of compute services, making them a versatile option for organizations with diverse workloads and evolving needs.

To effectively leverage Savings Plans, organizations should first determine their **baseline compute usage** and identify any opportunities for cost savings. This may involve right-sizing instances, consolidating workloads, or optimizing resource allocation. Once a baseline has been established, organizations can then select the appropriate Savings Plan type and commitment level to maximize their cost savings.

Both Reserved Instances and Savings Plans offer significant cost-saving potential for organizations looking to optimize their cloud financial operations. By carefully assessing their usage patterns, forecasting future needs, and regularly reviewing their commitments, organizations can achieve substantial cost reductions and improve their overall financial efficiency in the cloud.

The next section will discuss the importance of utilizing

automation and monitoring tools to further enhance cost optimization efforts and maintain financial control over cloud infrastructure.

Utilizing Automation and Monitoring Tools

In today's fast-paced and ever-evolving cloud landscape, businesses must be agile and proactive in managing their cloud finances. One of the most effective ways to achieve cost optimization is by leveraging **automation** and **monitoring tools**. These tools not only help in identifying potential cost savings but also ensure that your cloud infrastructure is running efficiently and securely. In this section, we will explore the various automation and monitoring tools available and how they can be utilized to optimize your cloud financial operations.

The Role of Automation in Cloud Finance

Automation is crucial in optimizing cloud costs by streamlining processes, reducing manual intervention, and minimizing human errors. By automating repetitive tasks, businesses can save time, resources, and money. Some of the key areas where automation can be applied in cloud finance include:

- **Infrastructure provisioning and de-provisioning:** Automating the process of creating and deleting resources based on demand can help avoid over-provisioning and reduce costs.
- **Auto-scaling:** Implementing auto-scaling policies can ensure that your infrastructure scales up or down based on actual usage, thereby optimizing resource allocation and minimizing costs.
- **Scheduled actions:** By automating scheduled actions, such as starting and stopping instances during non-business hours, businesses can save on costs incurred due to idle resources.

Monitoring Tools for Cost Optimization

Monitoring tools are vital in providing visibility into your cloud infrastructure, enabling you to track resource usage, performance, and costs. By leveraging these tools, businesses can gain insights into their cloud expenditure and identify areas for cost optimization. Some popular monitoring tools include:

- **Cloud provider-native tools:** Cloud service providers, such as AWS, Azure, and Google Cloud, offer built-in monitoring tools that provide insights into resource usage, performance, and costs. These tools, such as AWS Cost Explorer, Azure Cost Management, and Google Cloud Cost Tools, can help you analyze your cloud expenditure and identify cost-saving opportunities.
- **Third-party tools:** Several third-party tools, such as CloudHealth, CloudCheckr, and Cloudability, offer comprehensive cost management and optimization features. These tools provide advanced analytics, reporting, and recommendations to help businesses optimize their cloud spending.

Best Practices for Utilizing Automation and Monitoring Tools

In order to make the most of automation and monitoring tools, businesses should adopt the following best practices:

- Integrate automation and monitoring tools with your existing processes and workflows to ensure seamless operations.
- Regularly review and update automation policies and configurations to align with your evolving business needs and cloud infrastructure.
- Set up alerts and notifications to stay informed about any anomalies, cost spikes, or potential savings opportunities.

- Establish a culture of continuous improvement by regularly analyzing the data provided by monitoring tools and implementing cost optimization strategies.

Harnessing the Power of Automation and Monitoring Tools

In conclusion, automation and monitoring tools are essential components of a successful cloud finance strategy. By leveraging these tools, businesses can gain valuable insights into their cloud expenditure, identify cost-saving opportunities, and ensure that their cloud infrastructure runs efficiently and securely. By adopting a proactive approach to cost optimization and embracing the power of automation and monitoring tools, businesses can achieve financial efficiency in the cloud and maintain a competitive edge in today's digital landscape.

Achieving Financial Efficiency in the Cloud

In conclusion, achieving financial efficiency in the cloud is not only a desirable goal but a critical one for organizations seeking to maximize the value of their cloud investments. As we have explored throughout this chapter, there are several cost optimization strategies that can be employed to ensure that cloud financial operations are streamlined and cost-effective.

First and foremost, **understanding the importance of cost optimization** in cloud finance is crucial. This involves recognizing the unique challenges and opportunities the cloud environment presents and being proactive in addressing them. By staying informed and up-to-date on industry best practices, organizations can ensure they are well equipped to make informed decisions about their cloud financial operations.

Assessing and analyzing cloud expenditure is a vital step in the cost optimization process. This involves regularly reviewing and evaluating cloud usage and costs, identifying trends and patterns, and pinpointing areas where improvements can be made. By maintaining a clear and comprehensive understanding of their cloud spending, organizations can make data-driven decisions that lead to greater financial efficiency.

Implementing right-sizing and resource allocation strategies is another key aspect of cost optimization. This involves ensuring that cloud resources are appropriately matched to the organization's needs, avoiding both under-provisioning and over-provisioning. By regularly reviewing and adjusting resource allocation, organizations can minimize waste and ensure that they only pay for the resources they truly need.

Leveraging reserved instances and savings plans can also lead to significant cost savings. By committing to longer-term contracts and making upfront payments, organizations can secure lower rates for their cloud resources. This helps reduce overall expenditure and provides greater predictability and stability in terms of cloud costs.

Utilizing **automation and monitoring tools** is another essential component of cost optimization. These tools can help organizations to streamline their cloud financial operations, reducing the time and effort required to manage and optimize their cloud resources. By automating routine tasks and monitoring cloud usage in real time, organizations can quickly identify and address any issues that may be impacting their financial efficiency.

In summary, achieving financial efficiency in the cloud is a multifaceted process that requires a combination of strategic planning, ongoing monitoring, and proactive management. By employing the cost optimization strategies outlined in this chapter, organizations can ensure that they are making the most of their cloud investments and maximizing the value of their cloud-based resources. As the cloud continues to evolve and mature, organizations need to stay ahead of the curve and remain vigilant in their pursuit of financial efficiency and operational excellence.

Chapter Summary

- Cost optimization in cloud finance involves minimizing expenses associated with cloud-based financial operations while maintaining or improving performance, reliability, and security.
- Assessing and analyzing cloud expenditure is crucial for identifying inefficiencies and implementing strategic measures to reduce costs without compromising quality or functionality.
- Right-sizing and resource allocation strategies help ensure that cloud resources are appropriately matched to an organization's needs, avoiding both under-provisioning and over-provisioning.
- Leveraging reserved instances and savings plans can lead to significant cost savings by committing to longer-term contracts and making upfront payments.
- Utilizing automation and monitoring tools streamlines cloud financial operations, reduces manual intervention, and minimizes human errors.
- Integrating automation and monitoring tools with existing processes and workflows ensures seamless operations and better cost optimization.
- Regularly reviewing and updating automation policies, configurations, and resource allocation helps align with evolving business needs and cloud infrastructure.
- Achieving financial efficiency in the cloud requires a combination of strategic planning, ongoing monitoring, and proactive management, ensuring organizations maximize the value of their cloud investments.

7

INTEGRATING CLOUD FINANCIAL OPERATIONS WITH TRADITIONAL SYSTEMS

A futuristic cityscape where buildings are connected by beams of light, symbolizing cloud computing networks.

I n today's rapidly evolving financial landscape, businesses are increasingly recognizing the need to adapt and innovate to stay competitive. One of the most significant shifts in recent years has been the migration of financial operations to the cloud. Cloud financial operations offer numerous benefits, including increased efficiency, reduced costs, and enhanced security. However, many organizations still rely on traditional financial systems, either due to legacy infrastructure or a lack of understanding of the potential advantages of cloud-based solutions.

As a result, there is a growing need to **bridge the gap between cloud financial operations and traditional systems**, enabling businesses to harness the power of both approaches and create a more agile, streamlined financial infrastructure. This chapter will explore the challenges and opportunities associated with integrating cloud financial operations with traditional systems, offering practical strategies and real-world case studies to help businesses successfully navigate this complex transition.

We will begin by assessing the compatibility of cloud financial operations and traditional systems, examining the key differences and similarities between the two approaches, and identifying potential areas of synergy. Next, we will delve into strategies for seamless integration, discussing how businesses can effectively merge cloud-based and traditional financial processes to create a unified, efficient system.

In the following section, we will address the challenges that businesses may face when attempting to integrate cloud financial operations with traditional systems, offering practical solutions and guidance to overcome these obstacles. We will then present a series of case studies showcasing how established businesses have successfully integrated cloud financial operations into their existing infrastructure and the benefits they have experienced as a result.

Finally, we will conclude by reflecting on the future of finance, emphasizing the importance of embracing integrated cloud and traditional systems to remain competitive in an increasingly digital world. By understanding the nuances of cloud financial operations and traditional systems, businesses can make informed decisions about their financial infrastructure, ultimately driving growth and success in the modern marketplace.

Assessing the Compatibility of Cloud Financial Operations and Traditional Systems

Before diving into the integration of cloud financial operations and traditional systems, it is crucial to assess their compatibility. This section will provide a comprehensive guide to evaluating the compatibility of these two systems, ensuring a smooth transition and efficient integration.

Identifying the Key Components of Both Systems: The first step in assessing compatibility is to identify the key components of both cloud financial operations and traditional systems. This includes understanding the core functions, features, and processes of each system. For cloud financial operations, this may involve examining the **software-as-a-service (SaaS)** platforms, data storage and security, and real-time financial analytics. On the other hand, traditional systems may include legacy software, manual processes, and on-premise data storage.

Analyzing the Functional Requirements: Once the key components are identified, the next step is to analyze the functional requirements of both systems. This involves determining the essential functions that each system must perform to meet the organization's financial objectives. For example, both systems may need to support financial reporting, budgeting, and forecasting. By understanding these requirements, organizations can identify potential gaps or overlaps in functionality between the two systems.

Evaluating Data Compatibility: Data compatibility is critical in integrating cloud financial operations with traditional systems. Organizations must ensure that data can be seamlessly transferred between the two systems without loss or corruption. This may involve evaluating the data formats, structures, and protocols each system uses. Additionally, organizations should consider data security and privacy requirements, ensuring that sensitive financial information remains protected during the integration process.

Assessing System Scalability and Flexibility: As organizations grow and evolve, their financial systems must be able to adapt to changing needs. Therefore, it is essential to assess the scalability and flexibility of both cloud financial operations and traditional systems. Cloud-based systems typically offer greater scalability, as they can be easily expanded to accommodate increased data storage and processing needs. However, traditional systems may have limitations in terms of capacity and adaptability. By understanding these factors, organizations can make informed decisions about the best approach to integration.

Considering Cost Implications: Finally, organizations must consider the cost implications of integrating cloud financial operations with traditional systems. This includes evaluating the costs associated with software licensing, hardware upgrades, and data migration. Additionally, organizations should consider the potential cost savings that may result from increased efficiency, reduced manual processes, and improved financial analytics. By weighing these factors, organizations can determine the most cost-effective approach to integration.

In conclusion, assessing the compatibility of cloud financial operations and traditional systems is a critical step in the integration process. By carefully evaluating the key components, functional requirements, data compatibility, scalability, and cost implications, organizations can ensure a **seamless transition** and maximize the benefits of integrating these two systems.

Strategies for Seamless Integration of Cloud-Based and Traditional Financial Processes

The integration of cloud-based financial operations with traditional systems can be a complex process, but with the right strategies in place, businesses can achieve a seamless transition. This section will discuss various approaches to ensure a smooth integration of these two financial worlds.

Develop a Comprehensive Integration Plan: Before embarking on the integration process, it is crucial to develop a comprehensive plan that outlines the objectives, timelines, and resources required. This plan should include a **thorough analysis** of the existing traditional financial systems and processes, as well as the desired cloud-based solutions. By identifying the gaps and potential challenges, businesses can create a roadmap for successful integration.

Choose the Right Cloud Financial Solutions: Selecting the right cloud financial solutions is a critical factor in ensuring seamless integration. Businesses should evaluate various cloud-based tools and platforms based on their compatibility with existing systems, scalability, and ease of use. Additionally, it is essential to consider the security and compliance aspects of the chosen solutions to safeguard sensitive financial data.

Establish Clear Communication and Collaboration Channels: Effective communication and collaboration between the teams responsible for traditional and cloud-based financial operations are vital for successful integration. Establishing clear channels for sharing information, discussing challenges, and coordinating efforts will help to ensure that both sides are working towards the same goals.

Leverage APIs and Middleware Solutions: Application Programming Interfaces (APIs) and middleware solutions can play a crucial role in bridging the gap between cloud-based and traditional financial systems. These technologies enable the seamless exchange of data and information between different platforms, automating processes and reducing the risk of errors. By leveraging APIs and middleware, businesses can create a unified financial ecosystem that combines the best of both worlds.

Invest in Employee Training and Support: The integration of cloud financial operations with traditional systems may require employees to learn new skills and adapt to new processes. Investing in comprehensive training and ongoing support will help to ensure that employees are well-equipped to navigate the changes and contribute to the success of the integration.

Monitor and Optimize the Integration Process: Once the integration process is underway, it is essential to monitor its progress and make adjustments as needed. This may involve **refining the integration plan**, addressing unforeseen challenges, or optimizing the use of cloud-based solutions to maximize their benefits. Regular reviews and evaluations will help to ensure that the integration process remains on track and delivers the desired outcomes.

In conclusion, the seamless integration of cloud-based and traditional financial processes is achievable with the right strategies in place. By developing a comprehensive plan, choosing the right solutions, fostering communication and collaboration, leveraging APIs and middleware, investing in employee training, and monitoring the process, businesses can successfully navigate the transition and embrace the future of finance.

Overcoming Challenges in Merging Cloud Financial Operations with Traditional Systems

As businesses transition from traditional financial systems to cloud-based solutions, they are bound to face several challenges. However, with the right strategies and a proactive approach, organizations can successfully overcome these obstacles and reap the benefits of a seamlessly integrated financial ecosystem. In this section, we will discuss some common challenges and offer practical solutions for merging cloud financial operations with traditional systems.

Data Migration and Integration

One of the most significant challenges in merging cloud financial operations with traditional systems is the migration and integration of data. Organizations must ensure that all financial data is accurately transferred from their legacy systems to the cloud platform without any loss or discrepancies.

Solution: In order to overcome this challenge, businesses should develop a comprehensive data migration plan that includes a thorough assessment of data quality, mapping of data fields, and validation of migrated data. Additionally, organizations should consider using data integration tools that can automate the process and minimize the risk of errors.

Security and Compliance

Security and compliance concerns are paramount when dealing with financial data. Organizations must ensure their cloud financial operations adhere to the same security standards and regulatory requirements as their traditional systems.

Solution: To address security and compliance challenges, businesses should carefully evaluate the security features and certifications of their chosen cloud financial platform. Additionally, organizations should implement robust access controls, encryption, and monitoring tools to safeguard their financial data in the cloud.

Change Management and Employee Adoption

Merging cloud financial operations with traditional systems often requires significant changes in business processes and workflows. Employees may be resistant to adopting new technologies and may struggle to adapt to the new processes.

Solution: To facilitate a smooth transition, organizations should invest in comprehensive training and support programs to help employees understand the benefits of the new system and become proficient in using it. Additionally, businesses should involve key stakeholders in the planning and implementation process to ensure buy-in and support from all levels of the organization.

System Customization and Scalability

Traditional financial systems are often highly customized to meet the unique needs of an organization. Integrating these customizations with cloud financial operations can be challenging, as cloud platforms may not support the same level of customization.

Solution: To address this challenge, organizations should evaluate the flexibility and customization options offered by their chosen cloud financial platform. In some cases, businesses may need to reevaluate their customizations and adapt their processes to align with the capabilities of the cloud platform. Additionally, organizations should consider the scalability of the cloud platform to ensure that it can support their future growth and evolving needs.

Cost Management

While cloud financial operations can offer cost savings in the long run, the initial investment in migration and integration can be substantial. Organizations must carefully manage their budgets to **avoid overspending** during the transition.

Solution: To effectively manage costs, businesses should develop a detailed budget and timeline for the integration process, including expenses related to data migration, employee training, and system customization. Additionally, organizations should monitor their cloud usage and costs regularly to ensure that they are maximizing the value of their investment.

In conclusion, overcoming the challenges of merging cloud financial operations with traditional systems requires careful planning, collaboration, and a commitment to embracing change. By addressing these challenges head-on, organizations can successfully integrate their financial systems and position themselves for success in the rapidly evolving world of finance.

Case Studies: Successful Integration of Cloud Financial Operations in Established Businesses

In this section, we will explore real-life examples of established businesses that have successfully integrated cloud financial operations with their traditional systems. These case studies will provide valuable insights into the strategies and best practices employed by these organizations and the challenges they faced and overcame during the integration process.

Case Study 1: Global Retail Company

Our first case study involves a global retail company that operates both brick-and-mortar stores and a robust e-commerce platform. With a vast network of suppliers, employees, and customers, the company's financial operations were becoming increasingly complex and difficult to manage using their traditional financial systems.

To streamline its financial processes and improve efficiency, the company adopted a cloud-based financial management platform. The integration process involved the following steps:

- Identifying the key financial processes that could be migrated to the cloud, such as accounts payable, accounts receivable, and payroll.
- Selecting a cloud financial management solution that was compatible with the company's existing systems and could be easily integrated.
- Developing a detailed implementation plan, including a timeline for migrating each financial process to the cloud.
- Training employees on the new cloud-based platform and providing ongoing support during the transition period.
- Continuously monitoring and evaluating the performance of the integrated system to identify areas for improvement.

As a result of this successful integration, the retail company was able to significantly reduce manual data entry, improve the accuracy of financial reporting, and enhance overall operational efficiency.

Case Study 2: Manufacturing Firm

The second case study features a manufacturing firm that produces a wide range of products for various industries. The company's traditional financial systems struggled to keep up with the increasing volume of transactions and the growing complexity of its supply chain.

To address these challenges, the manufacturing firm implemented a cloud-based financial management system that could seamlessly integrate with its existing systems. The key steps in the integration process included:

- Conducting a thorough assessment of the company's financial processes to determine which could be effectively migrated to the cloud.
- Selecting a cloud financial management solution that met the company's specific needs and requirements.
- Developing a comprehensive integration plan, including a timeline for migrating each financial process to the cloud and a strategy for managing potential risks.
- Training employees on the new cloud-based platform and providing ongoing support to ensure a smooth transition.
- Regularly evaluating the performance of the integrated system to identify areas for improvement and optimize efficiency.

By successfully integrating cloud financial operations with its traditional systems, the manufacturing firm was able to achieve greater visibility into its financial data, streamline its supply chain management, and improve overall operational efficiency.

In conclusion, these case studies demonstrate that integrating cloud financial operations with traditional systems can yield significant benefits for established businesses. By carefully selecting the right cloud-based solution, developing a detailed implementation plan, and providing ongoing support for employees, organizations can successfully bridge the gap between cloud and traditional financial systems, paving the way for a more efficient and agile financial future.

Embracing the Future of Finance with Integrated Cloud and Traditional Systems

As we reach the end of our journey exploring the integration of cloud financial operations with traditional systems, it is essential to recognize the transformative potential this fusion holds for the future of finance. By **bridging the gap between these two worlds,** businesses can harness the power of cutting-edge cloud technology while maintaining the stability and familiarity of their existing financial systems. In this concluding section, we will recap the key insights gleaned from our exploration and emphasize the importance of embracing this integrated approach to finance.

Throughout this chapter, we have delved into the various aspects of integrating cloud financial operations with traditional systems, from assessing compatibility to overcoming challenges. We have learned that, although the process may seem daunting at first, numerous strategies and best practices can help businesses navigate this transition smoothly. By carefully evaluating the compatibility of cloud and traditional systems, organizations can identify the most effective ways to merge these two worlds and create a cohesive financial ecosystem.

Moreover, we have seen that the benefits of integrating cloud financial operations with traditional systems are manifold. By leveraging the agility, scalability, and real-time data capabilities of cloud technology, businesses can streamline their financial processes, improve decision-making, and ultimately drive growth. At the same time, maintaining a connection to traditional systems ensures that organizations can continue to rely on the tried-and-true methods that have served them well in the past.

In our exploration of case studies, we have witnessed firsthand the transformative impact that integrated cloud and traditional financial systems can have on established businesses. These real-world examples serve as powerful reminders that, with the right approach and mindset, organizations can successfully navigate the challenges of integration and emerge stronger and more competitive than ever before.

As we look to the future of finance, it is clear that the integration of cloud financial operations with traditional systems will play an increasingly critical role in shaping the industry landscape. As more and more businesses recognize the value of this integrated approach, we can expect to see a growing number of innovative solutions and best practices emerge to facilitate this transition. By staying abreast of these developments and embracing the fusion of cloud and traditional systems, businesses can position themselves at the forefront of the financial revolution.

In conclusion, integrating cloud financial operations with traditional systems represents a significant opportunity for businesses to enhance their financial processes and drive growth. By embracing this integrated approach, organizations can harness the best of both worlds and chart a course toward a more efficient, agile, and data-driven future. As we continue to witness the rapid evolution of the finance industry, businesses need to remain adaptable and open to change, ensuring that they are well-equipped to navigate the challenges and opportunities that lie ahead.

Chapter Summary

- The integration of cloud financial operations with traditional systems is essential for businesses to remain competitive in the rapidly evolving financial landscape.
- Assessing compatibility between cloud and traditional systems involves evaluating key components, functional requirements, data compatibility, scalability, and cost implications.
- Strategies for seamless integration include developing a comprehensive plan, choosing the right cloud financial solutions, establishing clear communication channels, leveraging APIs and middleware, investing in employee training, and monitoring the integration process.
- Common challenges in merging cloud financial operations with traditional systems include data migration and

integration, security and compliance, change management and employee adoption, system customization and scalability, and cost management.

- Overcoming these challenges requires careful planning, collaboration, and a commitment to embracing change.
- Real-world case studies demonstrate the transformative impact of integrating cloud financial operations with traditional systems, leading to improved efficiency, decision-making, and growth.
- The future of finance will increasingly rely on the integration of cloud and traditional systems, with innovative solutions and best practices emerging to facilitate this transition.
- Embracing the fusion of cloud and traditional financial systems allows businesses to harness the best of both worlds, positioning themselves at the forefront of the financial revolution and ensuring adaptability to future challenges and opportunities.

8

BEST PRACTICES FOR IMPLEMENTING CLOUD FINANCIAL SOLUTIONS

An image illustrating the seamless integration of cloud-based financial systems with various devices.

I n today's fast-paced and ever-evolving business landscape, organizations of all sizes constantly seek ways to streamline their operations, reduce costs, and improve overall efficiency. One area that has seen significant growth and innovation in recent years is the realm of **cloud financial solutions**. These cutting-edge tools and platforms have revolutionized the way businesses manage their finances, offering a host of benefits such as increased accessibility, real-time data analysis, and seamless integration with other essential systems.

As an author and industry expert, I have witnessed firsthand the transformative impact that cloud financial solutions can have on an organization's bottom line. However, I also understand that implementing these solutions can be a complex and daunting task, particularly for those who may be new to the world of cloud computing. That's why I have dedicated this chapter to providing you with a comprehensive guide to implementing cloud financial solutions, complete with best practices, tips, and insights gleaned from my years of experience in the field.

In this chapter, we will explore the process of evaluating and selecting the right cloud financial solution for your business, ensuring that you make an informed decision that aligns with your organization's unique needs and goals. We will also delve into the critical steps involved in developing a comprehensive implementation plan, from establishing a clear timeline and budget to identifying potential risks and challenges that may arise during the transition.

Data security and compliance are paramount when it comes to cloud financial operations, and we will discuss the best practices for safeguarding your sensitive financial data in the cloud. Additionally, we will examine the importance of training and supporting your team throughout the implementation process, ensuring a smooth and successful transition to your new cloud financial solution.

By the end of this chapter, you will be well-equipped with the knowledge and tools necessary to maximize the benefits of cloud financial solutions for your organization. So, let's embark on this exciting journey together and unlock the full potential of cloud-based financial operations for your business.

Evaluating and Selecting the Right Cloud Financial Solution for Your Business

In today's rapidly evolving business landscape, choosing the right cloud financial solution is crucial for the success and growth of your organization. However, with numerous options available in the market, it can be overwhelming to determine which solution best aligns with your business needs and objectives. This section will discuss the key factors to consider when evaluating and selecting the right cloud financial solution for your business.

Identify your business needs and objectives: Before diving into the world of cloud financial solutions, you must clearly understand your organization's specific needs and objectives. This includes assessing your current financial processes, identifying areas for improvement, and determining the desired outcomes from implementing a cloud financial solution. By having a clear vision of your organization's goals, you can better evaluate the features and capabilities of various cloud financial solutions.

Evaluate the features and functionality: When comparing different cloud financial solutions, it is important to assess the features and functionality offered by each platform. Some key features to consider include the following:

- Integration capabilities: Ensure that the solution seamlessly integrates with your existing systems, such as ERP, CRM, and other business applications.
- Scalability: The solution should be able to grow with your business, allowing for easy expansion and adaptation to changing business needs.
- Customization: The platform should offer a high degree of customization to fit your organization's unique requirements and processes.

- Reporting and analytics: Robust reporting and analytics capabilities are essential for gaining insights into your financial operations and making data-driven decisions.

Assess the vendor's reputation and track record: The credibility and reliability of the cloud financial solution provider are crucial factors to consider. Research the vendor's reputation in the industry, their track record of successful implementations, and the level of support and resources they offer to their clients. Look for customer testimonials and case studies to gain insights into the experiences of other organizations that have implemented the solution.

Consider the total cost of ownership: When evaluating cloud financial solutions, it is essential to consider the upfront costs and ongoing expenses associated with the platform. This includes subscription fees, implementation costs, training expenses, and any additional costs for customization or integration. Be sure to compare the total cost of ownership for each solution to ensure you are making a cost-effective decision for your organization.

Test the solution through a demo or trial: Before making a final decision, it is highly recommended to test the cloud financial solution through a demo or trial period. This will allow you to experience the platform's features and functionality firsthand, as well as assess its ease of use and compatibility with your organization's processes. Additionally, this will provide an opportunity to engage with the vendor's support team and gauge their responsiveness and expertise.

In conclusion, selecting the right cloud financial solution for your business requires careful consideration of various factors, including your organization's needs and objectives, the features and functionality of the platform, the vendor's reputation and track record, the total cost of ownership, and the ability to test the solution through a demo or trial. By thoroughly evaluating these aspects, you can confidently choose a cloud financial solution that will drive efficiency, streamline processes, and ultimately contribute to the success and growth of your organization.

Developing a Comprehensive Implementation Plan

A successful transition to a cloud financial solution requires a well-thought-out and comprehensive implementation plan. This plan serves as a roadmap, guiding your organization through each step of the process, from initial evaluation to post-implementation support. This section will discuss the key components of an effective implementation plan and provide practical tips to help you create a plan that sets your organization up for success.

Define your objectives and goals: The first step in developing an implementation plan is to clearly define your objectives and goals. What do you hope to achieve by implementing a cloud financial solution? Your goals may include improved efficiency, cost savings, better data security, or increased scalability. Be specific and measurable in your goal-setting, as this will help you track progress and determine the success of your implementation.

Assemble a cross-functional implementation team: Your implementation team should include representatives from all relevant departments, such as finance, IT, and operations. This ensures that all perspectives are considered and that the needs of each department are addressed during the implementation process. Additionally, appoint a project manager to oversee the team and ensure that tasks are completed on time and within budget.

Identify key milestones and deadlines: Break down the implementation process into smaller tasks and assign deadlines for each task. This will help you track progress and ensure that the project stays on schedule. Key milestones may include selecting a cloud financial solution, migrating data, configuring the system, and training employees.

Develop a data migration strategy: Migrating your financial data to the cloud is critical to the implementation process. Work with your IT department and cloud financial solution provider to develop a **data migration strategy** that ensures data integrity and minimizes downtime. This may involve cleaning and validating your data, mapping data fields between your current system and the new solution, and testing the migration process.

Plan for system configuration and customization: Most cloud financial solutions offer a degree of customization to meet your organization's unique needs. Identify any required customizations and work with your solution provider to configure the system accordingly. This may include setting up user roles and permissions, configuring workflows and approval processes, and integrating with other software applications.

Develop a training and support plan: In order to ensure a smooth transition, it is essential to provide comprehensive training and support for your employees. Develop a training plan that covers all aspects of the new system, from basic navigation to advanced features. To accommodate different learning styles and schedules, consider offering multiple training formats, such as in-person workshops, webinars, and self-paced online courses. Additionally, **establish a support system** to address any questions or issues that arise during and after the implementation process.

Monitor progress and adjust as needed: Regularly review your implementation plan and track progress against your defined milestones and deadlines. Be prepared to adjust your plan as needed to address any challenges or changes in circumstances. This may involve reallocating resources, revising deadlines, or modifying your training plan.

In conclusion, a comprehensive implementation plan is essential for a successful transition to a cloud financial solution. By defining clear objectives, assembling a cross-functional team, and carefully planning each step of the process, you can ensure a smooth implementation that maximizes the benefits of cloud financial solutions for your organization.

Ensuring Data Security and Compliance in Cloud Financial Operations

In today's digital age, **data security and compliance** have become paramount concerns for businesses of all sizes. As organizations increasingly adopt cloud financial solutions, it is crucial to ensure that these platforms provide robust security measures and adhere to relevant regulatory standards. This section will discuss the key aspects of data security and compliance in cloud financial operations, offering practical guidance for safeguarding your organization's sensitive financial information.

Understanding the Importance of Data Security and Compliance

Financial data is among the most sensitive and valuable information held by any organization. Unauthorized access, data breaches, or non-compliance with regulatory requirements can lead to severe financial losses, reputational damage, and legal penalties. Therefore, it is essential to prioritize data security and compliance when implementing cloud financial solutions.

Assessing the Security Features of Cloud Financial Solutions

When evaluating cloud financial solutions, it is crucial to examine the security features offered by each platform. Key aspects to consider include the following:

- **Data encryption:** Ensure that the solution provides strong encryption for data at rest and in transit, using industry-standard algorithms and protocols.
- **Access controls:** Look for a platform that offers granular access controls, allowing you to define user roles and permissions based on your organization's needs.
- **Multi-factor authentication (MFA):** MFA adds an extra layer of security by requiring users to provide two or more

forms of identification before accessing the system.
- **Regular security updates and patches:** Choose a provider that is committed to maintaining the security of their platform by promptly addressing vulnerabilities and releasing updates.

Ensuring Compliance with Regulatory Requirements

Depending on your industry and location, your organization may be subject to various financial regulations and standards. In order to maintain compliance, it is essential to select a cloud financial solution that supports the necessary regulatory requirements. Key compliance aspects to consider include the following:

- Data residency: Some regulations require financial data to be stored within specific geographic boundaries. Ensure that your chosen solution can accommodate these requirements.
- Audit trails: Look for a platform that offers comprehensive audit trails, enabling you to track and monitor all activities within the system for compliance purposes.
- Reporting capabilities: Ensure the solution provides the necessary reporting tools to meet your organization's regulatory reporting obligations.

Developing a Data Security and Compliance Strategy

Implementing a robust data security and compliance strategy is essential for mitigating risks and ensuring the successful adoption of cloud financial solutions. Key steps in developing this strategy include:

- Conducting a thorough risk assessment: Identify potential threats and vulnerabilities in your cloud financial operations and develop appropriate mitigation measures.
- Establishing clear policies and procedures: Develop comprehensive policies and procedures that outline your

organization's approach to data security and compliance in the cloud.

- Regularly reviewing and updating your strategy: As the threat landscape and regulatory environment evolve, it is crucial to periodically review and update your data security and compliance strategy to ensure its continued effectiveness.

Collaborating with Your Cloud Financial Solution Provider

A strong partnership with your cloud financial solution provider is essential for ensuring data security and compliance. Work closely with your provider to:

- Understand their security and compliance capabilities: Gain a clear understanding of the provider's security features and compliance support, and ensure they align with your organization's requirements.
- Establish a shared responsibility model: Clearly define the responsibilities of both your organization and the provider in maintaining data security and compliance.
- Monitor and address emerging threats and vulnerabilities: Collaborate with your provider to stay informed about new threats and vulnerabilities, and develop strategies to address them effectively.

By prioritizing data security and compliance in your cloud financial operations, you can confidently embrace the benefits of these solutions while safeguarding your organization's sensitive financial information.

Training and Supporting Your Team for a Smooth Transition

As you embark on the journey of implementing a cloud financial solution for your organization, it is crucial to recognize that the success of this transition largely depends on the people who will be using the system daily. Your team members are the backbone of your organization, and their ability to adapt to the new cloud financial solution will directly impact the overall efficiency and effectiveness of your operations. This section will discuss the importance of providing comprehensive training and support to your team members, ensuring a smooth and seamless transition to the new system.

First, it is essential to acknowledge that change can be challenging, especially when adopting new technologies. Your team members may have varying levels of familiarity and comfort with cloud-based systems, and it is your responsibility as a leader to **create an environment that fosters learning and growth.** By providing the necessary resources, guidance, and encouragement, you can empower your team to embrace the new cloud financial solution with confidence and enthusiasm.

Here are some best practices for training and supporting your team during the transition to a cloud financial solution:

Communicate the benefits: Start by clearly communicating the reasons behind the transition and its benefits to the organization. Help your team understand how the new system will streamline processes, improve efficiency, and ultimately contribute to the company's growth and success. This will create a sense of ownership and motivation among team members, making them more receptive to learning and adopting the new system.

Develop a tailored training program: Recognize that each team member may have different learning needs and preferences. Develop a training program that caters to these individual requirements, incorporating a mix of learning methods such as classroom sessions, online tutorials, hands-on workshops, and one-on-one coaching. This will ensure that everyone has the opportunity to learn at their own pace and in a manner that suits them best.

Provide ongoing support: The learning process does not end once the initial training is completed. It is essential to provide ongoing support to your team members as they navigate the new system and encounter challenges along the way. **Establish a dedicated support team** or point of contact that team members can reach out to for assistance, and encourage open communication and collaboration among team members to share knowledge and best practices.

Monitor progress and gather feedback: Regularly assess the progress of your team members in adopting the new cloud financial solution and solicit their feedback on the training and support provided. This will help you identify areas where additional training or resources may be needed and adjust accordingly to ensure a successful transition.

Celebrate successes: Recognize and celebrate the achievements of your team members as they master the new system. This not only boosts morale but also reinforces the positive impact of the cloud financial solution on the organization.

In conclusion, the key to a smooth transition to a cloud financial solution lies in the **effective training and support** of your team members. By investing in their growth and development, you will ensure the successful adoption of the new system and create a culture of continuous learning and improvement that will benefit your organization in the long run.

Maximizing the Benefits of Cloud Financial Solutions for Your Organization

In conclusion, the successful implementation of cloud financial solutions can bring about a myriad of benefits for your organization. From streamlining processes and reducing costs to enhancing data security and compliance, these solutions have the potential to revolutionize the way your business manages its financial operations. However, to truly maximize these benefits, following the **best practices** outlined in this chapter is crucial.

First and foremost, it is essential to **evaluate and select the right cloud financial solution** that aligns with your organization's unique needs and objectives. By conducting thorough research and considering factors such as scalability, integration capabilities, and vendor reputation, you can ensure that your chosen solution will support your business's growth and success in the long run.

Developing a comprehensive implementation plan is another critical step in the process. This plan should outline the necessary tasks, timelines, and resources required to ensure a smooth transition to the new system. By setting clear expectations and milestones, you can keep your team on track and minimize disruptions to your daily operations.

Data security and compliance should never be an afterthought when implementing cloud financial solutions. By working closely with your chosen vendor and your internal IT team, you can establish robust security measures and protocols that protect your organization's sensitive financial data. Regular audits and monitoring can also help you maintain compliance with relevant regulations and industry standards.

Training and supporting your team is another essential component of a successful implementation. By providing your employees with the necessary resources, guidance, and ongoing support, you can empower them to adapt to the new system and leverage its full potential. This, in turn, will help your organization reap the benefits of increased efficiency, improved decision-making, and enhanced collaboration.

In summary, implementing cloud financial solutions can be a game-changer for your organization, but only if you follow the best practices outlined in this chapter. By selecting the right solution, developing a solid implementation plan, ensuring data security and compliance, and supporting your team throughout the transition, you can maximize the benefits of cloud financial solutions and set your organization on a path to continued success.

Chapter Summary

- Cloud financial solutions can revolutionize the way businesses manage their finances, offering benefits such as increased accessibility, real-time data analysis, and seamless integration with other systems.
- Selecting the right cloud financial solution requires evaluating factors such as business needs, features and

functionality, vendor reputation, the total cost of ownership, and the ability to test the solution through a demo or trial.

- Developing a comprehensive implementation plan is crucial for a successful transition to a cloud financial solution, including defining objectives, assembling a cross-functional team, identifying milestones, and planning for data migration and system configuration.

- Data security and compliance are paramount in cloud financial operations, and organizations must assess the security features of cloud financial solutions, ensure compliance with regulatory requirements, and develop a data security and compliance strategy.

- Training and supporting the team during the transition to a cloud financial solution is essential for a smooth implementation, including communicating the benefits, developing a tailored training program, providing ongoing support, and monitoring progress.

- A strong partnership with the cloud financial solution provider is vital for ensuring data security and compliance, including understanding their security and compliance capabilities, establishing a shared responsibility model, and collaborating to address emerging threats and vulnerabilities.

- Celebrating successes and recognizing the achievements of team members as they master the new system can boost morale and reinforce the positive impact of the cloud financial solution on the organization.

- By following the best practices outlined in this chapter, organizations can maximize the benefits of cloud financial solutions, leading to increased efficiency, improved decision-making, and enhanced collaboration.

9

CASE STUDIES: SUCCESSFUL CLOUD FINANCIAL OPERATIONS TRANSFORMATIONS

An image of a serene cloud-filled sky, with the clouds shaped like different financial tools and resources.

I n today's rapidly evolving business landscape, organizations are constantly seeking ways to improve efficiency, reduce costs, and drive innovation. One area that has seen significant transformation in recent years is **financial operations**. As companies look to modernize their financial processes and systems, many are turning to cloud-based solutions to help them achieve these goals. In this chapter, we will explore the power of cloud financial operations transformations through a series of real-world case studies, showcasing how organizations across various industries have successfully harnessed the potential of cloud technology to revolutionize their financial operations.

Cloud financial operations, also known as cloud finance or cloud-based financial management, refers to the use of cloud computing technology to manage and streamline an organization's financial processes. This includes accounting, budgeting, financial planning, and reporting tasks. By leveraging the power of the cloud, organizations can access a range of benefits, including increased agility, improved scalability, enhanced security, and reduced operational costs.

The case studies presented in this chapter will demonstrate how organizations from different sectors – fintech, retail, healthcare, and manufacturing – have successfully transformed their financial operations by adopting cloud-based solutions. These examples will highlight the unique challenges faced by each organization, the strategies they employed to overcome these challenges, and the impressive results they achieved due to their cloud financial operations transformation.

As we delve into these case studies, it is important to recognize that each organization's journey to cloud financial operations is unique, and there is no one-size-fits-all approach to achieving success. However, by examining the experiences of others, we can identify common themes and best practices that can help guide organizations as they embark on their own cloud financial operations transformation journey.

At the conclusion of this chapter, we will summarize the key takeaways from these case studies and discuss the future outlook for cloud financial operations transformations. As more organizations recognize the benefits of cloud-based financial management, we expect continued growth and innovation in this area, ultimately leading to more efficient, agile, and competitive businesses in the global marketplace.

Embracing Agility: A Fintech Company's Journey to Cloud Financial Operations

In today's fast-paced and ever-evolving financial landscape, **agility is the key to success.** This section will delve into the journey of a fintech company that embraced cloud financial operations to achieve unparalleled agility, enabling them to stay ahead of the curve and maintain a competitive edge.

The fintech company, which we will refer to as **FinTechX**, began as a small start-up with a mission to revolutionize the financial services industry. It aimed to provide innovative solutions to both businesses and consumers, leveraging cutting-edge technology to streamline processes and enhance the overall customer experience. However, as FinTechX grew, it realized that its traditional, on-premise financial systems were holding it back. The lack of flexibility and scalability hindered its ability to adapt to the rapidly changing market conditions and customer demands.

Recognizing the need for a more agile and scalable solution, FinTechX embarked on a journey to transform its financial operations by migrating to the cloud. The company's leadership team understood that this transition would enable them to stay competitive and drive innovation and growth.

The first step in FinTechX's journey was to identify the right cloud-based financial management platform that would cater to their unique needs. After a thorough evaluation of various solutions, they chose a platform that offered robust functionality, seamless integration with their existing systems, and the ability to scale as the company grew.

The implementation process was carefully planned and executed, with a focus on minimizing disruption to the company's day-to-day operations. FinTechX's finance team worked closely with the cloud solution provider to ensure a smooth transition, addressing any challenges that arose along the way.

Once the cloud-based financial management system was in place, FinTechX began to reap the benefits of its transformation. The company experienced significant improvements in efficiency as manual processes were automated and data were consolidated into a single, easily accessible platform. This allowed the finance team to focus on more strategic tasks, such as analyzing data to identify trends and opportunities for growth.

Moreover, the cloud-based system enabled FinTechX to scale its financial operations easily. As the company expanded into new markets and added new products and services, the system could be quickly adapted to accommodate these changes. This agility proved invaluable in helping FinTechX maintain a competitive edge in the fast-paced fintech industry.

The move to cloud financial operations also fostered a culture of innovation within the company. With access to real-time data and advanced analytics capabilities, FinTechX's finance team could provide valuable insights to the rest of the organization. This data-driven approach helped the company identify new opportunities, optimize existing processes, and ultimately drive growth.

In conclusion, FinTechX's journey to cloud financial operations demonstrates the power of embracing agility in today's dynamic business environment. By adopting a cloud-based financial management system, the company could streamline processes, drive innovation, and scale with ease. This transformation enabled FinTechX to stay competitive in the fintech industry and set the stage for continued success in the future.

Streamlining Processes: How a Retail Giant Optimized Their Financial Operations

In today's fast-paced and competitive business environment, retail giants constantly seek ways to optimize their financial operations and stay ahead of the curve. One such retail giant, with a global presence and thousands of stores, recognized the need to streamline their financial processes and embarked on a transformative journey towards cloud financial operations. This section will delve into the steps taken by this retail behemoth and the remarkable results it achieved through the power of cloud financial operations.

The retail giant's initial financial operations were characterized by a complex web of legacy systems, manual processes, and a lack of real-time visibility into financial data. This led to inefficiencies, increased operational costs, and hindered the company's ability to make informed, data-driven decisions. Recognizing the need for change, the company's leadership adopted a cloud-based financial operations platform to streamline processes, improve visibility, and drive growth.

The first step in this transformation was to thoroughly assess the company's existing financial processes and identify areas for improvement. This involved engaging with various stakeholders, including finance teams, store managers, and supply chain partners, to gain a comprehensive understanding of the challenges and inefficiencies faced by the organization.

Armed with this knowledge, the retail giant partnered with a leading cloud financial operations solution provider to design and implement a tailored, scalable, and secure platform that would address its unique needs. The platform enabled the company to automate manual processes, such as invoice processing and expense management, and provided real-time access to financial data across the organization.

One of the key features of the cloud financial operations platform was its ability to integrate seamlessly with the company's existing systems, including its ERP, CRM, and supply chain management solutions. This integration allowed for a single source of truth for financial data, eliminating the need for manual reconciliation and reducing the risk of errors.

The retail giant also leveraged the power of advanced analytics and artificial intelligence (AI) capabilities offered by the cloud platform. This enabled them to gain deeper insights into their financial performance, identify trends and patterns, and make data-driven decisions to optimize their operations further.

The results of this transformation were nothing short of remarkable. The retail giant experienced a significant reduction in operational costs, with a **30% decrease in manual processes** and a **25% reduction in the time taken to close their financial books**. The company also saw a marked improvement in decision-making, with real-time access to financial data empowering store managers and finance teams to make informed choices that drove growth and profitability.

In conclusion, the retail giant's journey toward cloud financial operations is a powerful testament to the transformative potential of such solutions. By streamlining processes, improving visibility, and leveraging advanced analytics, the company was able to optimize its financial operations and position itself for continued success in an increasingly competitive landscape. This case study inspires other organizations looking to harness the power of cloud financial operations to drive growth, efficiency, and innovation.

Driving Innovation: A Healthcare Organization's Transformation through Cloud Financial Operations

The healthcare industry is no stranger to innovation, with advancements in medical technology and patient care occurring rapidly. However, the financial operations side of healthcare organizations has often lagged behind in embracing new technologies. This section will explore how one healthcare organization successfully transformed its financial operations by adopting cloud-based solutions, ultimately driving innovation and improving patient outcomes.

The Challenge: Outdated Financial Systems and Inefficient Processes

The healthcare organization, a large hospital network, faced numerous challenges with its existing financial systems and processes. Its legacy systems were outdated, siloed, and lacked the flexibility to adapt to the ever-changing healthcare landscape. This led to inefficient processes, increased manual work, and limited visibility into financial performance. Additionally, the organization struggled to keep up with regulatory compliance and reporting requirements, putting them at risk for financial penalties and reputational damage.

The Solution: Implementing a Cloud-Based Financial Operations Platform

Recognizing the need for a more agile and scalable financial operations solution, the healthcare organization embarked on a journey to transform its financial operations by implementing a **cloud-based platform**. The platform offered a comprehensive suite of tools and features, including financial planning and analysis, revenue cycle management, and regulatory compliance management.

The implementation process began with a thorough assessment of the organization's existing financial processes and systems, identifying areas for improvement and opportunities for innovation. Next, the organization worked closely with the cloud financial operations platform provider to develop a customized solution tailored to their unique needs and requirements.

The Results: Improved Efficiency, Enhanced Visibility, and a Culture of Innovation

The healthcare organization's transformation through cloud financial operations yielded **impressive results**. By streamlining processes and automating manual tasks, the organization significantly reduced the time and effort required for financial planning, analysis, and reporting. This allowed their finance team to focus on more strategic initiatives, such as identifying cost-saving opportunities and optimizing resource allocation.

The cloud-based platform also provided the organization with enhanced visibility into its financial performance, enabling it to make data-driven decisions and better manage its revenue cycle. This led to improved cash flow and a stronger financial position, allowing the organization to invest in new technologies and patient care initiatives.

Perhaps most importantly, the adoption of cloud financial operations fostered a culture of innovation within the organization. The finance team became more agile and adaptable, embracing new technologies and best practices to drive continuous improvement. This mindset extended beyond the finance department, with other areas of the organization also adopting innovative solutions to improve patient care and operational efficiency.

The successful transformation of this healthcare organization's financial operations through cloud-based solutions demonstrates the power of embracing innovation in the finance function. By adopting a cloud financial operations platform, the organization could streamline processes, enhance visibility into financial performance, and foster a **culture of innovation**. This ultimately led to improved patient outcomes and a stronger financial position, showcasing the potential for cloud financial operations to drive meaningful change in the healthcare industry.

Global Expansion: A Manufacturing Company's Success with Cloud-Based Financial Operations

In today's rapidly evolving global marketplace, manufacturing companies face unique challenges in managing their financial operations. As they expand their operations across borders, they must navigate complex regulatory environments, manage multiple currencies, and adapt to diverse business practices. In this section, we will explore how a leading manufacturing company successfully harnessed the power of cloud-based financial operations to fuel its global expansion.

The company, a multinational manufacturer of high-tech components, had been experiencing rapid growth and was poised to enter new markets. However, its legacy financial systems struggled to keep pace with the increasing complexity and scale of its operations. The company's finance team was burdened with manual processes, data silos, and a lack of real-time visibility into financial performance.

Recognizing the need for a more agile and scalable solution, the company embarked on a journey to transform its financial operations through **cloud technology.**

The first step in its transformation was selecting a cloud-based financial management platform that could **support its global operations.** It chose a solution that offered robust multi-currency capabilities, streamlined regulatory compliance, and seamless integration with its existing ERP systems. This platform also provided advanced analytics and reporting tools, enabling the finance team to gain real-time insights into their financial performance across all markets.

With the new cloud-based system in place, the company could automate many of its manual processes, such as accounts payable and receivable, expense management, and financial reporting. This reduced the risk of errors and freed up valuable time for the finance team to focus on more strategic initiatives. Additionally, the platform's multi-currency capabilities allowed the company to easily manage transactions in various currencies, minimizing the impact of currency fluctuations on their bottom line.

One of the most significant benefits of the cloud-based financial operations transformation was the company's ability to scale its operations **quickly and efficiently.** As they entered new markets, the finance team could easily onboard new entities and adapt to local regulations without the need for costly and time-consuming system customizations. This agility enabled the company to accelerate its global expansion and maintain a competitive edge in the marketplace.

Furthermore, the cloud-based platform facilitated greater collaboration between the finance team and other departments within the company. With real-time access to financial data, teams across the organization could make more informed decisions, driving innovation and operational efficiency. This cross-functional collaboration was instrumental in helping the company achieve its strategic growth objectives.

In conclusion, the manufacturing company's success with cloud-based financial operations demonstrates the transformative potential of this technology. By embracing a cloud-based solution, the company was able to streamline processes, drive innovation, and accelerate its global expansion. As more organizations recognize the benefits of cloud financial operations, we can expect to see a growing number of success stories like this one, shaping the future of finance in the global marketplace.

Key Takeaways and Future Outlook for Cloud Financial Operations Transformations

As we have seen throughout this chapter, cloud financial operations have the potential to revolutionize the way businesses manage their finances, streamline processes, and drive innovation. We have gained valuable insights into the transformative power of cloud financial operations by examining the case studies of a fintech company, a retail giant, a healthcare organization, and a manufacturing company. In this conclusion, we will recap the key takeaways from these case studies and discuss the future outlook for cloud financial operations transformations.

Key Takeaways

Agility and Flexibility: Cloud financial operations enable businesses to be more agile and flexible, as demonstrated by the fintech company's journey. By adopting cloud-based solutions, organizations can quickly adapt to changing market conditions and scale their operations with ease.

Process Optimization: The retail giant's success in streamlining its financial operations highlights the importance of process optimization. Cloud financial operations can help businesses automate manual tasks, reduce errors, and improve overall efficiency.

Innovation and Collaboration: The healthcare organization's transformation showcases the power of cloud financial operations in driving innovation and collaboration. By leveraging cloud-based tools, businesses can foster a culture of innovation and improve decision-making through real-time data access and collaboration.

Global Expansion: The manufacturing company's global expansion demonstrates the potential of cloud financial operations in supporting international growth. Cloud-based solutions can help businesses navigate complex regulatory environments and manage multiple currencies, making it easier to expand into new markets.

Future Outlook

As more businesses recognize the benefits of cloud financial operations, we expect a continued shift towards cloud-based solutions in the financial industry. This transformation will likely be driven by several factors, including the following:

Technological Advancements: As technology continues to evolve, we can expect to see even more sophisticated and powerful cloud-based financial tools become available. These advancements will further enhance the capabilities of cloud financial operations, making them an increasingly attractive option for businesses of all sizes.

Regulatory Compliance: As governments and regulatory bodies around the world continue to update their requirements for financial reporting and data security, businesses will need to adapt their financial operations accordingly. Cloud-based solutions can help organizations stay compliant with these ever-changing regulations, making them an essential component of future financial operations.

Growing Adoption: As more businesses adopt cloud financial operations, we expect to see a snowball effect, with even more organizations following suit. This growing adoption will likely lead to increased competition among cloud-based financial solution providers, driving innovation and improvements in the industry.

Integration with Other Technologies: As businesses continue to embrace digital transformation, we can expect to see increased integration between cloud financial operations and other emerging technologies, such as artificial intelligence, machine learning, and blockchain. This integration will further enhance the capabilities of cloud financial operations, making them an even more valuable tool for businesses.

In conclusion, the future of cloud financial operations is bright, with significant potential for growth and innovation. By embracing this transformation, businesses can unlock new levels of efficiency, agility, and innovation, positioning themselves for success in an increasingly competitive global marketplace.

Chapter Summary

- Cloud financial operations offer increased agility and flexibility, allowing organizations to adapt quickly to changing market conditions and scale their operations with ease, as demonstrated by the fintech company's journey.
- Process optimization is a key benefit of cloud financial operations, as shown by the retail giant's success in streamlining its financial processes. Automation of manual tasks, reduction of errors, and improved efficiency are some of the advantages.
- Cloud financial operations can drive innovation and collaboration within organizations, as illustrated by the healthcare organization's transformation. Real-time data access and collaboration enabled by cloud-based tools foster a culture of innovation and better decision-making.
- Cloud financial operations can support global expansion, as demonstrated by the manufacturing company's success in expanding its operations internationally. Cloud-based solutions help businesses navigate complex regulatory environments and manage multiple currencies.
- Technological advancements will continue to enhance the capabilities of cloud financial operations, making them an increasingly attractive option for businesses of all sizes.
- Regulatory compliance is a driving factor for the adoption of cloud financial operations, as cloud-based solutions can help organizations stay compliant with ever-changing regulations.

- Growing adoption of cloud financial operations will lead to increased competition among solution providers, driving innovation and improvements in the industry.
- Integration with other emerging technologies, such as artificial intelligence, machine learning, and blockchain, will further enhance the capabilities of cloud financial operations, making them an even more valuable tool for businesses.

10

THE FUTURE OF CLOUD FINANCIAL OPERATIONS

A futuristic cityscape where buildings are connected by beams of light, symbolizing cloud computing networks.

The world of finance has always been a dynamic and ever-changing landscape, and the advent of cloud technology has only accelerated this transformation. As we stand at the precipice of a new era in financial operations, it is crucial for businesses and individuals alike to embrace the evolution of cloud financial operations and prepare for the exciting opportunities and challenges that lie ahead.

The concept of cloud computing has revolutionized the way we store, access, and process data. It has enabled organizations to scale their operations, streamline processes, and reduce costs while maintaining high security and compliance. In finance, cloud technology has opened up new avenues for **innovation, efficiency, and growth.** By leveraging the power of the cloud, financial institutions can harness cutting-edge tools and technologies to optimize their operations and deliver better services to their clients.

In this chapter, we will explore the future of cloud financial operations and delve into the key trends and developments that are shaping this rapidly evolving landscape. From the rise of artificial intelligence and machine learning to the game-changing potential of blockchain technology, we will examine the factors driving change in the world of cloud finance. We will also discuss the impact of regulatory changes and compliance on cloud financial operations and the critical role of cybersecurity in safeguarding these systems.

As we embark on this journey into the future of cloud financial operations, it is essential to keep an open mind and be prepared to adapt to the changes that are unfolding before our eyes. By staying informed and proactive, businesses and individuals can position themselves to thrive in this dynamic and innovative environment, harnessing the power of the cloud to unlock new levels of success and prosperity. So, let us begin our exploration of the future of cloud financial operations and discover the exciting possibilities that await us in this brave new world of finance.

The Rise of Artificial Intelligence and Machine Learning in Cloud Finance

The world of finance has always been a fertile ground for technological innovation, and the advent of cloud computing has only accelerated this trend. As we move further into the *21st century*, the role of **artificial intelligence (AI) and machine learning (ML)** in cloud financial operations is becoming increasingly significant. These cutting-edge technologies have the potential to revolutionize the way businesses manage their finances, offering unprecedented levels of **efficiency, accuracy, and insight.**

AI and ML are often used interchangeably, but they are distinct concepts. AI refers to the broader idea of machines or computers mimicking human intelligence, while ML is a subset of AI that focuses on the ability of machines to learn and improve from experience without being explicitly programmed. In the context of cloud finance, both AI and ML play crucial roles in automating tasks, analyzing data, and making predictions.

One of the most significant benefits of incorporating AI and ML into cloud financial operations is the **automation of repetitive and time-consuming tasks.** By leveraging intelligent algorithms, businesses can automate various processes such as invoice processing, expense management, and financial reporting. This saves time and resources and reduces the risk of human error, ensuring that financial data is accurate and up-to-date.

Another key advantage of AI and ML in cloud finance is their **ability to analyze vast amounts of data quickly and efficiently.** Financial operations generate a wealth of information, and harnessing this data can provide valuable insights into a company's financial health and performance. AI-powered analytics tools can process and interpret complex data sets, identifying patterns and trends that would be difficult or impossible for humans to detect. This enables businesses to make more informed decisions, optimize their financial strategies, and ultimately drive growth and profitability.

Predictive analytics is another area where AI and ML are making a significant impact on cloud financial operations. By analyzing historical data and identifying patterns, machine learning algorithms can predict future financial outcomes, such as cash flow, revenue, and expenses. This allows businesses to anticipate potential challenges and opportunities, enabling them to plan more effectively and make strategic decisions based on data-driven insights.

However, the rise of AI and ML in cloud finance also presents challenges, particularly in terms of data privacy and security. As businesses increasingly rely on these technologies to manage their financial operations, they must also ensure that sensitive financial data is protected from unauthorized access and potential breaches. This highlights the importance of robust cybersecurity measures and a strong focus on data governance in the age of AI-driven cloud finance.

In conclusion, the rise of artificial intelligence and machine learning in cloud financial operations is transforming the way businesses manage their finances. By automating tasks, analyzing data, and making predictions, these technologies offer unprecedented levels of efficiency, accuracy, and insight, enabling companies to thrive in an increasingly competitive and complex financial landscape. As we look to the future, businesses need to embrace these innovations and adapt to the evolving world of cloud finance while also addressing the challenges and risks of this new era of technological advancement.

Blockchain Technology: A Game Changer for Financial Operations

The world of finance has always been a breeding ground for innovation and technological advancements. One such groundbreaking technology that has been making waves in recent years is **blockchain**. Often associated with cryptocurrencies like Bitcoin, blockchain technology has the potential to revolutionize the way financial operations are conducted in the cloud. In this section, we will explore the transformative power of blockchain technology and how it is poised to reshape the landscape of cloud financial operations.

At its core, blockchain is a decentralized, digital ledger that records transactions across a network of computers. This distributed nature of the technology ensures that no single entity has control over the data, making it highly secure and transparent. The use of cryptography further enhances the security of the system, as each block in the chain contains a unique code that links it to the previous block. This makes it virtually impossible to tamper with the data without altering the entire chain, which would require an enormous amount of computing power.

Now, let's delve into the ways blockchain technology can revolutionize cloud financial operations:

Enhanced Security and Fraud Prevention: The decentralized and tamper-proof nature of blockchain technology makes it an ideal solution for securing financial transactions in the cloud. By eliminating the need for a central authority, blockchain reduces the risk of fraud and cyberattacks, ensuring that financial data remains secure and accurate.

Faster and Cost-effective Transactions: Traditional financial transactions often involve multiple intermediaries, which can lead to delays and increased costs. Blockchain technology enables peer-to-peer transactions, cutting out the intermediaries and allowing for faster, more cost-effective financial operations. This can be particularly beneficial for cross-border transactions, where fees and processing times can be significantly reduced.

Improved Data Integrity and Transparency: The transparent nature of blockchain technology ensures that all parties involved in a transaction have access to the same information. This not only improves data integrity but also **fosters trust among stakeholders**. In cloud financial operations, this can lead to a more efficient collaboration between different departments and organizations and better decision-making based on accurate, real-time data.

Streamlined Compliance and Auditing: Regulatory compliance is a critical aspect of financial operations, and blockchain technology can simplify this process by providing an immutable record of transactions. This makes it easier for organizations to track and verify their compliance with various regulations and for auditors to review financial records with **greater accuracy and efficiency.**

Smart Contracts: One of the most promising applications of blockchain technology in finance is the use of smart contracts. These are self-executing contracts with the terms of the agreement directly written into code. Smart contracts can automate various financial processes, such as payments and settlements, reducing the need for manual intervention and increasing operational efficiency.

In conclusion, blockchain technology has the potential to be a game changer for cloud financial operations. By offering enhanced security, faster transactions, improved data integrity, streamlined compliance, and the possibility of smart contracts, blockchain can significantly transform the way financial operations are conducted in the cloud. As we move towards a future where technology continues to play a pivotal role in the finance industry, embracing blockchain technology will be crucial for organizations looking to stay ahead of the curve and capitalize on its benefits.

The Impact of Regulatory Changes and Compliance on Cloud Financial Operations

As cloud financial operations continue to evolve, organizations need to stay informed about the latest regulatory changes and compliance requirements. With the increasing adoption of cloud-based services, regulatory bodies worldwide are continually updating their guidelines to ensure the safety and security of financial data. In this section, we will explore the impact of these regulatory changes on cloud financial operations and discuss the importance of maintaining compliance in this ever-changing landscape.

The Growing Importance of Regulatory Compliance

In the era of digital transformation, regulatory compliance has become a critical aspect of cloud financial operations. As more organizations migrate their financial systems to the cloud, they must adhere to various regulations to protect sensitive financial data and maintain the integrity of their operations. These regulations are designed to mitigate risks associated with data breaches, fraud, and other security threats that could compromise the financial stability of an organization.

Key Regulatory Changes Affecting Cloud Financial Operations

Several regulatory changes have a direct impact on cloud financial operations, including the following:

General Data Protection Regulation (GDPR): This European Union regulation has set a new standard for data privacy and protection, requiring organizations to implement robust security measures to safeguard personal data. Cloud financial service providers must ensure their platforms are GDPR-compliant to avoid hefty fines and reputational damage.

Payment Services Directive 2 (PSD2): This EU directive aims to create a more integrated and secure European payments market by promoting innovation and competition. It requires financial institutions to provide third-party access to customer data, which has significant implications for cloud financial operations, including the need for enhanced security measures and data-sharing capabilities.

Sarbanes-Oxley Act (SOX): This US legislation requires public companies to maintain accurate financial records and establish internal controls to prevent fraud. Cloud financial service providers must ensure their platforms meet SOX requirements, including data retention, access controls, and audit trails.

Strategies for Maintaining Compliance in Cloud Financial Operations

To navigate the complex regulatory landscape and maintain compliance, organizations should consider the following strategies:

Partner with a reputable cloud service provider: Choose a provider with a proven track record of compliance and a deep understanding of the regulatory environment. Ensure they have the necessary certifications and attestations to demonstrate their commitment to security and compliance.

Implement robust security measures: Adopt a comprehensive approach to security, including encryption, multi-factor authentication, and intrusion detection systems. Regularly review and update security policies to keep pace with evolving threats and regulatory requirements.

Conduct regular audits and assessments: Perform periodic assessments of your cloud financial operations to identify potential compliance gaps and vulnerabilities. Engage third-party auditors to validate your compliance posture and provide recommendations for improvement.

Stay informed about regulatory changes: Keep abreast of the latest regulatory developments and updates to ensure your organization remains compliant. Participate in industry forums and engage with regulatory bodies to stay informed about best practices and emerging trends.

Embracing Compliance as a Competitive Advantage

In the rapidly evolving world of cloud financial operations, regulatory compliance is not just a legal obligation but a competitive advantage. Organizations that proactively address regulatory changes and maintain a robust compliance posture will be better positioned to mitigate risks, protect sensitive financial data, and build trust with customers and stakeholders. In addition, by embracing compliance as a strategic priority, organizations can unlock new opportunities for growth and innovation in the dynamic landscape of cloud finance.

The Role of Cybersecurity in Safeguarding Cloud Financial Operations

As cloud financial operations continue to evolve and become more sophisticated, so do the threats that aim to compromise the integrity and security of these systems. As a result, **cybersecurity** has become an essential aspect of safeguarding cloud financial operations, ensuring that sensitive data and transactions are protected from unauthorized access, theft, and manipulation. In this section, we will delve into the importance of cybersecurity in cloud finance and explore the strategies and tools that can be employed to maintain a secure environment.

The Growing Importance of Cybersecurity in Cloud Finance

The shift towards cloud-based financial operations has brought numerous advantages, including increased efficiency, cost savings, and scalability. However, this transition also presents new challenges in terms of data security and privacy. In addition, cybercriminals are constantly devising new ways to exploit vulnerabilities in cloud systems, making it crucial for organizations to prioritize cybersecurity measures.

Data breaches and cyberattacks can have severe consequences for businesses, including financial losses, reputational damage, and regulatory penalties. In cloud financial operations, the stakes are even higher, as sensitive financial data and transactions are at risk. This makes it imperative for organizations to invest in robust cybersecurity measures to protect their cloud-based financial systems.

Strategies and Tools for Safeguarding Cloud Financial Operations

To ensure the security of cloud financial operations, organizations must adopt a comprehensive approach that encompasses multiple layers of protection. Some key strategies and tools to consider include the following:

Encryption: Encrypting data, both at rest and in transit, is a fundamental aspect of safeguarding sensitive financial information. By using **strong encryption algorithms**, organizations can ensure that even if data is intercepted or accessed by unauthorized parties, it remains unreadable and secure.

Access Control: Implementing strict access control measures prevents unauthorized access to cloud financial systems. This includes using multi-factor authentication, role-based access control, and regular audits of user privileges to ensure that only authorized personnel can access sensitive data and perform critical operations.

Intrusion Detection and Prevention: Deploying advanced intrusion detection and prevention systems can help organizations identify and respond to potential threats in real time. These tools monitor network traffic and system activities for signs of malicious activity, enabling swift action to mitigate potential risks.

Security Information and Event Management (SIEM): SIEM solutions collect, analyze, and correlate security event data from various sources, providing organizations with a comprehensive view of their security posture. By leveraging SIEM tools, businesses can detect and respond to potential threats more effectively, ensuring the security of their cloud financial operations.

Regular Security Assessments: Conducting regular security assessments, including vulnerability scanning and penetration testing, can help organizations identify and address potential weaknesses in their cloud financial systems. These assessments should be performed by qualified professionals and should be an integral part of an organization's overall cybersecurity strategy.

Employee Training and Awareness: Human error remains one of the most significant contributors to security breaches. Providing regular training and raising awareness about cybersecurity best practices can help employees recognize and avoid potential threats, thereby reducing the risk of successful cyberattacks.

In conclusion, the role of cybersecurity in safeguarding cloud financial operations cannot be overstated. As the landscape of cloud finance continues to evolve, organizations must remain vigilant and proactive in their approach to security. By implementing robust cybersecurity measures and staying abreast of emerging threats and technologies, businesses can ensure the safety and integrity of their cloud-based financial systems, paving the way for a secure and prosperous future in cloud finance.

Preparing for a Dynamic and Innovative Future in Cloud Finance

As we reach the end of our exploration into the world of cloud financial operations, it is evident that the future holds immense potential for innovation, efficiency, and growth. The rapid advancements in technology and the ever-changing regulatory landscape present challenges and opportunities for businesses and financial professionals alike. In this concluding chapter, we will recap the key takeaways and provide insights on how to prepare for a dynamic and innovative future in cloud finance.

The integration of artificial intelligence and machine learning into cloud financial operations has the potential to revolutionize the way businesses manage their finances. By automating repetitive tasks, reducing human error, and providing real-time insights, these technologies can significantly enhance the efficiency and accuracy of financial processes. To harness the full potential of AI and machine learning, organizations must invest in the necessary infrastructure, upskill their workforce and embrace a culture of continuous learning and adaptation.

Blockchain technology, with its decentralized and secure nature, has the potential to transform financial operations by streamlining processes, reducing fraud, and increasing transparency. As more organizations adopt blockchain-based solutions, **businesses must stay informed** about the latest developments and explore the potential applications of this technology in their financial operations.

Regulatory changes and compliance requirements will continue to shape the future of cloud financial operations. As governments and regulatory bodies adapt to the evolving landscape, organizations must remain vigilant and proactive in ensuring compliance with relevant regulations. This includes staying informed about the latest regulatory updates, investing in robust compliance management systems, and fostering a culture of accountability and transparency.

Cybersecurity is of paramount importance in safeguarding cloud financial operations. As cyber threats become more sophisticated, businesses must prioritize the protection of their financial data and systems. This involves implementing robust security measures, conducting regular risk assessments, and fostering a culture of cybersecurity awareness among employees.

In conclusion, the future of cloud financial operations is both exciting and challenging. To thrive in this dynamic environment, businesses and financial professionals must be adaptable, forward-thinking, and proactive in embracing new technologies and practices. By staying informed, investing in the right tools and infrastructure, and fostering a culture of innovation and continuous learning, organizations can navigate the complexities of the evolving financial landscape and unlock new opportunities for growth and success.

Chapter Summary

- Cloud technology has revolutionized the finance industry, offering new avenues for innovation, efficiency, and growth.
- Artificial intelligence and machine learning are transforming cloud financial operations by automating tasks, analyzing data, and making predictions, leading to increased efficiency and accuracy.
- Blockchain technology has the potential to revolutionize cloud financial operations by enhancing security, enabling faster transactions, improving data integrity, and streamlining compliance and auditing processes.
- Regulatory changes and compliance requirements play a critical role in shaping the future of cloud financial operations, making it essential for organizations to stay informed and proactive in ensuring compliance.
- Cybersecurity is paramount in safeguarding cloud financial operations, requiring businesses to prioritize protecting their financial data and systems.
- To thrive in the dynamic environment of cloud finance, businesses and financial professionals must be adaptable,

forward-thinking, and proactive in embracing new technologies and practices.

- Staying informed, investing in the right tools and infrastructure, and fostering a culture of innovation and continuous learning are crucial for organizations to navigate the complexities of the evolving financial landscape.
- By embracing the evolution of cloud financial operations, businesses can unlock new opportunities for growth and success in the rapidly changing world of finance.

EMBRACING THE CLOUD FOR
FINANCIAL SUCCESS

In today's rapidly evolving business landscape, organizations constantly seek innovative ways to streamline operations, optimize resources, and drive growth. One of the most significant developments in recent years has been the widespread adoption of cloud computing, which has revolutionized the way businesses manage their IT infrastructure and deliver services. As a result, cloud-based financial solutions have emerged as a powerful tool for organizations to transform their financial operations and achieve greater efficiency, agility, and scalability.

The journey to **cloud financial operations is not a one-size-fits-all approach** but a strategic and well-planned process that requires a deep understanding of the organization's unique needs, goals, and challenges. This journey begins with a clear vision of the desired outcomes and a commitment to embracing the cloud as a catalyst for change. It involves assessing the current state of the organization's financial operations, identifying opportunities for improvement, and selecting the right cloud-based solutions that align with the organization's objectives.

This book has explored the various aspects of cloud financial operations, including the key benefits, challenges, and future trends. We have also delved into best practices for successful cloud adoption and provided insights into how organizations can leverage the power of the cloud to achieve financial success. As we conclude our journey, we must reflect on the lessons learned and the steps organizations can take to embrace the cloud for financial success.

In this final chapter, we will summarize the main takeaways from our exploration of cloud financial operations and provide a roadmap for organizations to follow as they embark on their journey to the cloud. We will discuss the importance of developing a strategic plan, overcoming challenges and mitigating risks, staying ahead of future trends, and adopting best practices for successful cloud implementation. Ultimately, our goal is to empower organizations with the knowledge and tools they need to harness the full potential of cloud-based financial solutions and pave the way for a more prosperous and sustainable future in the cloud era.

Key Benefits of Cloud-Based Financial Solutions

As we embark on the journey to cloud financial operations, it is essential to understand the key benefits that cloud-based financial solutions bring to the table. These benefits not only streamline financial processes but also contribute to the overall financial success of organizations. This section will delve into the most significant advantages of adopting cloud-based financial solutions.

Cost Efficiency: One of the most compelling benefits of cloud-based financial solutions is cost efficiency. By leveraging the cloud, organizations can significantly reduce their capital expenditure on IT infrastructure, software licenses, and hardware maintenance. The pay-as-you-go model of cloud services allows businesses to scale their financial operations according to their needs, ensuring that they only pay for the resources they consume. This flexibility translates into substantial cost savings, especially for small and medium-sized enterprises.

Enhanced Accessibility and Collaboration: Cloud-based financial solutions enable users to access critical financial data and applications from anywhere, at any time, and on any device. This enhanced accessibility **empowers employees to work remotely** and collaborate more efficiently with their colleagues, partners, and clients. Real-time data sharing and seamless integration with other cloud-based applications further streamline financial processes, leading to improved decision-making and faster response times.

Improved Security and Compliance: Contrary to popular belief, cloud-based financial solutions **provide better security** than traditional on-premise systems. Cloud service providers invest heavily in advanced security measures, including encryption, multi-factor authentication, and regular security audits. Additionally, they ensure compliance with industry-specific regulations and standards, such as GDPR, HIPAA, and PCI DSS. By entrusting their financial data to reputable cloud providers, organizations can mitigate the risk of data breaches and focus on their core business activities.

Scalability and Flexibility: As organizations grow and evolve, their financial operations must adapt to changing business requirements. Cloud-based financial solutions offer unparalleled scalability and flexibility, allowing businesses to expand or downsize their financial operations with ease. This adaptability ensures that organizations can respond to market fluctuations and seize new opportunities without being constrained by rigid, outdated systems.

Automation and Innovation: Cloud-based financial solutions often come equipped with advanced automation features, such as **artificial intelligence (AI) and machine learning (ML)** capabilities. These cutting-edge technologies enable organizations to automate routine financial tasks, such as data entry, invoicing, and reporting, thereby increasing efficiency and reducing the risk of human error. Furthermore, cloud providers continuously innovate and update their offerings, ensuring that businesses have access to the latest tools and technologies to stay ahead of the competition.

In conclusion, cloud-based financial solutions offer a myriad of benefits that can significantly contribute to an organization's financial success. By embracing these advantages, businesses can optimize their financial operations, reduce costs, and stay agile in today's fast-paced, ever-evolving market landscape.

Overcoming Challenges and Mitigating Risks

As with any significant technological shift, adopting cloud-based financial solutions comes with its own set of challenges and risks. However, with the right strategies and a proactive approach, organizations can effectively overcome these hurdles and reap the full benefits of cloud financial operations. In this section, we will discuss some of the most common challenges and risks associated with cloud adoption and provide practical guidance on how to mitigate them.

Data Security and Privacy: One of the primary concerns when transitioning to cloud-based financial solutions is the security and privacy of sensitive financial data. To address this challenge, organizations should carefully evaluate the security measures and protocols offered by cloud service providers. This includes ensuring the provider complies with relevant industry standards and regulations, such as the **General Data Protection Regulation (GDPR)** and the **Payment Card Industry Data Security Standard (PCI DSS)**. Additionally, organizations should implement robust internal security policies and practices, such as data encryption, multi-factor authentication, and regular security audits.

Compliance and Regulatory Requirements: Compliance with industry-specific regulations and standards is another critical aspect of cloud financial operations. Organizations must ensure that their chosen cloud service provider complies with all relevant regulations and can provide the necessary documentation and support during audits. It is also essential for organizations to stay up-to-date with the latest regulatory changes and adapt their cloud-based financial processes accordingly.

Integration with Existing Systems: Integrating cloud-based financial solutions with existing on-premise systems can be a complex and time-consuming process. To overcome this challenge, organizations should develop a comprehensive integration plan that outlines the necessary steps and resources required for a seamless transition. This may involve working closely with the cloud service provider, leveraging APIs and integration tools, and investing in employee training to ensure a smooth and efficient integration process.

Vendor Lock-In and Flexibility: Vendor lock-in is a potential risk when adopting cloud-based financial solutions, as it may limit an organization's ability to switch providers or return to on-premise solutions if needed. To mitigate this risk, organizations should carefully **evaluate the flexibility and interoperability** of the cloud services they choose. This may include selecting a provider that offers open standards and APIs, as well as considering multi-cloud or hybrid cloud strategies to avoid over-reliance on a single vendor.

Managing Costs and ROI: While cloud-based financial solutions can offer significant cost savings in the long run, organizations must carefully manage their cloud spending to ensure a positive return on investment (ROI). This includes monitoring and optimizing cloud resource usage, negotiating favorable contract terms with cloud service providers, and regularly reviewing cloud costs to identify potential savings opportunities.

In conclusion, overcoming the challenges and mitigating the risks associated with cloud financial operations requires a strategic and proactive approach. By addressing these concerns head-on and implementing best practices, organizations can confidently embrace the cloud and unlock its full potential for financial success.

Future Trends in Cloud Financial Operations

As we continue to navigate the ever-evolving landscape of cloud financial operations, it is crucial to stay informed about the emerging trends that will shape the future of this industry. By understanding and adapting to these trends, businesses can remain **competitive and agile** in the face of constant change. In this section, we will explore some of the most significant trends that are expected to impact cloud financial operations in the coming years.

Artificial Intelligence and Machine Learning: One of the most transformative trends in cloud financial operations is the integration of **artificial intelligence (AI) and machine learning (ML)** technologies. These advanced tools are revolutionizing the way businesses analyze and process financial data, enabling them to make more informed decisions and streamline their operations. AI and ML can be used to automate repetitive tasks, identify patterns and anomalies in financial data, and even predict future trends. As these technologies become more sophisticated, we can expect to see even greater levels of automation and efficiency in cloud financial operations.

Real-Time Data Processing and Analysis: Accessing and analyzing financial data in real time is becoming increasingly important for businesses that want to stay ahead of the competition. Cloud-based financial solutions enable organizations to process and analyze data more quickly than ever, providing them with up-to-date insights that can inform strategic decision-making. In the future, we can expect to see even more advanced tools for real-time data processing and analysis, allowing businesses to react more swiftly to changes in the market and capitalize on emerging opportunities.

Enhanced Security and Compliance: As the volume of financial data being stored and processed in the cloud continues to grow, so does the need for robust security and compliance measures. In the coming years, we can expect significant advancements in the security features offered by cloud-based financial solutions, including more sophisticated encryption methods, advanced threat detection, and improved access controls. Additionally, as regulatory requirements evolve, cloud financial operations providers must ensure their platforms comply with the latest standards and best practices.

Increased Adoption of Blockchain Technology: Blockchain technology has the potential to revolutionize many aspects of financial operations, including payment processing, supply chain management, and contract execution. As more businesses begin to explore the benefits of blockchain, we expect to see increased adoption of this technology within cloud financial operations. This will likely lead to greater transparency, reduced fraud, and more efficient processes across the board.

Greater Integration and Interoperability: As cloud financial operations mature, we can expect greater levels of integration and interoperability between different platforms and systems. This will enable businesses to share data more easily and collaborate with partners, suppliers, and customers, ultimately leading to more streamlined and efficient operations. Additionally, as more organizations adopt cloud-based financial solutions, we expect to see **increased standardization** and the development of industry-wide best practices.

In conclusion, the future of cloud financial operations is both exciting and full of potential. By staying informed about these emerging trends and adapting to the changing landscape, businesses can ensure they are well-positioned to capitalize on the many benefits cloud-based financial solutions offer. As we continue to embrace the cloud for financial success, the possibilities for innovation and growth are virtually limitless.

Best Practices for Successful Cloud Adoption

As we have explored throughout this book, adopting cloud-based financial solutions can bring significant benefits to your organization. However, to ensure a smooth and successful transition, it's crucial to follow best practices that will help you navigate the challenges and mitigate risks. This section will discuss some of the most effective strategies for adopting cloud financial operations.

Develop a clear cloud strategy: Before embarking on your cloud journey, it's essential to have a well-defined strategy that outlines your organization's goals, objectives, and expected outcomes. This should include a thorough assessment of your current financial systems, processes, and infrastructure to identify areas that can benefit from cloud-based solutions. By having a clear roadmap, you can ensure that your cloud adoption efforts are aligned with your overall business objectives.

Choose the right cloud provider and solution: With numerous cloud providers and solutions available in the market, selecting the right one for your organization can be daunting. It's essential to conduct thorough research and evaluate different providers based on factors such as security, scalability, integration capabilities, and cost. Additionally, consider the specific needs of your financial operations and choose a solution that offers the features and functionality required to support your processes.

Prioritize data security and compliance: Data security and regulatory compliance are critical concerns for any organization, especially when dealing with sensitive financial information. Ensure your chosen cloud provider adheres to industry-standard security protocols and complies with relevant regulations such as GDPR, HIPAA, or PCI DSS. Implement robust access controls, encryption, and monitoring tools to safeguard your financial data in the cloud.

Plan for a phased migration: Transitioning to cloud-based financial operations can be a complex process, and it's essential to approach it in a phased manner. Start by migrating less critical applications and processes to the cloud, and gradually move more complex and mission-critical systems as you gain confidence in your cloud infrastructure. This approach allows you to identify and address any issues or challenges that may arise during the migration process, minimizing disruption to your business operations.

Invest in employee training and change management: The success of your cloud adoption efforts largely depends on the ability of your employees to adapt to new systems and processes. Therefore, provide **comprehensive training and support** to help your team understand the benefits of cloud-based financial solutions and how to use them effectively. Additionally, implement a robust change management strategy to address any resistance or concerns that may arise during the transition.

Monitor and optimize your cloud environment: Once your financial operations are up and running in the cloud, it's essential to continuously monitor and optimize your environment to ensure optimal performance, cost-efficiency, and security. Regularly review your cloud usage, identify areas for improvement, and make necessary adjustments to your infrastructure and processes. This will help you maximize the benefits of your cloud investment and drive long-term financial success.

By following these best practices, your organization can successfully embrace cloud-based financial solutions and unlock the full potential of cloud financial operations. As you embark on this journey, remember that the path to financial success in the cloud era is an ongoing process that requires continuous learning, adaptation, and innovation. Embrace the opportunities and challenges that lie ahead, and you'll be well on your way to achieving greater efficiency, agility, and growth in your financial operations.

Final Thoughts: The Path to Financial Success in the Cloud Era

As we reach the end of our journey through the world of cloud financial operations, it is essential to take a moment to reflect on the key takeaways and insights that have been shared throughout this book. The cloud has revolutionized the way businesses manage their financial operations, offering a **plethora of benefits** that can propel organizations toward financial success. However, as with any technological advancement, it is crucial to approach the cloud with a strategic mindset and a clear understanding of the challenges and risks involved.

The cloud era has brought forth a new wave of opportunities for businesses to streamline their financial processes, enhance collaboration, and make data-driven decisions. By leveraging the power of cloud-based financial solutions, organizations can achieve greater efficiency, cost savings, and scalability, all while maintaining a high level of security and compliance. The key to unlocking these benefits lies in **understanding your organization's unique requirements** and **selecting the right cloud solution** that aligns with your goals and objectives.

Overcoming the challenges and mitigating the risks associated with cloud adoption requires a proactive approach and a commitment to continuous improvement. By staying informed about the latest trends and best practices in cloud financial operations, businesses can confidently navigate the complexities of the cloud landscape. It is essential to invest in employee training, establish robust governance frameworks, and foster a culture of collaboration and innovation to ensure a smooth transition to the cloud.

As we look to the future, it is clear that the **cloud will continue to play a pivotal role in shaping the financial operations landscape.** With *emerging technologies* such as artificial intelligence, machine learning, and blockchain poised to further disrupt the industry, organizations must remain agile and adaptable to stay ahead of the curve. By embracing these advancements and integrating them into their cloud-based financial operations, businesses can unlock new levels of efficiency, accuracy, and insight.

In conclusion, the path to financial success in the cloud era is paved with both opportunities and challenges. By adopting a strategic approach, staying informed, and embracing the latest trends and best practices, organizations can harness the full potential of cloud-based financial solutions and drive their businesses toward a prosperous future. As we close this chapter, we hope that the insights and guidance provided throughout this book will serve as a valuable resource for your organization as you embark on your journey to cloud financial operations success.

ABOUT THE AUTHOR

Peter Bates is a prolific author and leading expert in the field of digital finance. With a passion for exploring the intersection of finance and technology, Peter has dedicated his career to understanding and simplifying complex topics for readers worldwide. His acclaimed *"Digital Finance"* series has garnered praise for its insightful analysis and practical guidance on embracing innovation in the financial sector.

With a background in finance, technology, and education, Peter has the unique ability to break down complex subjects into easily digestible concepts for readers of all levels. His work has helped countless professionals navigate the rapidly changing landscape of digital finance, and his continued dedication to the field promises many more valuable insights in the future.

As Peter continues to expand his Digital Finance series, his commitment to providing accessible and informative resources for finance and technology enthusiasts remains unwavering. Stay tuned for more groundbreaking books from this thought leader in the world of digital finance.

Printed in Poland
by Amazon Fulfillment
Poland Sp. z o.o., Wrocław

30778676R00096